Permanent Passenger: My Life on a Cruise Ship

Permanent Passenger: My Life on a Cruise Ship

by Micha Berman

Permanent Passenger:
My Life on a Cruise Ship

Cover design by Geoff Wagner
Book design/layout by Media Solutions, San Francisco

ISBN 978-1-4357-0618-7

Printed in the United States of America

To My Parents – More loving guides I could not have asked for.

To Charol – my wife and love of my life.
(Honey, please don't read the fifth chapter.)

Author's Note

This book is about my personal journey. It is not a book about the cruise line industry, Carnival Cruise Lines, Pekingese dogs, how to find love, or one million ways to make a billion dollars before you turn fifteen. My life on the cruise ship took place in the early 1990's. The world has changed since then, and that includes cruise ships. They are bigger, better, more beautiful and now have these strange things called internet cafes. I love the cruise line industry and all the people I worked with; well, maybe most of them. My story is not meant to harm, hurt, disable, or make anyone cry. Again this is my personal journey; it may be uncouth, politically incorrect, wacky, perverted, illogical, whimsical and disgusting, but I am not sure if I mentioned it already—this is my personal journey. Enjoy and get some diapers on.

Table of Contents

Chapter 1   Project Random...3

Chapter 2   Love at First Sight 17

Chapter 3   Man on the Mike...27

Chapter 4   Separate Lives 37

Chapter 5   Is There Love on the Love Boat?.........................51

Chapter 6   Ports, Ports, and More Ports 69

                     Photo Section 81

Chapter 7   Temptations of the Sea 89

Chapter 8   Moments of Crisis...97

Chapter 9   Honeymoon Blues 111

Chapter 10   Is There Life After Cruising? 115

Ten Commandments of Cruise Life......................................121

Addendum: Materials from the Job Search 123

Chapter 1
Project Random

I had no idea what I wanted to be when I grew up; my biggest dilemma was—I was grown up! Like many college students in their senior year I had imagined a thousand different opportunities for myself ranging from law school to medical school; I even considered the prepackaged backpacking tour across Europe. I had frequent panic attacks when I realized in several months I would be wearing a black cap and gown, marching among a wave of young ambitious faces. An even stranger vision was seeing myself in a white T-shirt with the words, "I'M LOST" emblazoned on it while running through the crowd indiscriminately firing a machine gun. Time was ticking and I had an idea. I would do something radical; this was no time for ordinary measures. I would lock myself up in my room for seven days with Richard Nelson Bolles' *What Color Is Your Parachute* and conduct my own brainstorming session.

College had been relatively easy up to this point. I had always received good grades and was your typical student, a member of a fraternity, involved in student government and of course a fan of David Letterman. As my friends headed off to Florida and to ski resorts for winter vacation I remained to read my bible. The silence on campus created a perfect setting for my meditation. One of the first exercises in Bolles' book was to write your own autobiography, something I had hoped someone else would do when I was long dead. I realized through this writing that ever

3

since I was a child I had been entertaining groups of people. I was the ubiquitous jester, the one responsible for entertaining when the teachers weren't looking. My greatest claim to fame involved a seventh grade incident in which I spat into the music teacher's coffee cup without her ever knowing. This was enough to gain the respect of my classmates and by the time I graduated high school I was awarded the highest honor of all at the senior awards ceremony—"class clown." If I hadn't been able to make others laugh I may have easily become a target of the schoolyard bullies due to my emaciated physique. I have always been thin, and at times I have been compared to a stick. My body wasn't going to get me much attention so I relied on my personality. My older brother didn't fare much better; with ears the size of Dumbo, he was often surrounded by fellow schoolmates and taunted with the painful yell, "BIG EARS."

I developed a list of requirements for the job I would seek. I was looking for a nontraditional job in a creative atmosphere that would allow me to speak to crowds, be around young people and travel at the same time. Several friends suggested I look into the travel industry and in particular the cruise industry, which was one of its hottest sectors. I had stumbled upon the pot of gold at the end of the rainbow.

My basic knowledge of cruise ships at this point in my life was comparable to the typical American. I was a scholar of the Saturday evening television hit the *Love Boat*. Images of love affairs at sea and murder plots filled my mind when I heard the word "cruising." The truth was Americans didn't know very much about cruising. Only 5% of the American public have ever been on a cruise. How many times do you come across people who have worked on a cruise ship? But I still had the *Love Boat* to work with. Having no intention of serving drinks like Isaac nor any illusions of becoming a doctor or captain, I narrowed my choices down to gopher the purser and Julie the cruise director. Gopher was just too goofy. I had arrived at a very scary conclusion: I wanted to become Julie McCoy.

Yet, I knew instinctively I had found the perfect match. All cruise ships have 'cruise staff', the entertainers and personnel who run the activities. These are the people who greet passengers as they arrive on a cruise ship as well as entertain and host all the fun events on board like bingo, shuffleboard and dance contests. I began to imagine the job. I pictured myself on a ship sailing into the crimson sunset, surrounded by exotic women and fruity tropical drinks. My mouth began to water, a good sign indeed. It was time to begin searching for my dream position.

Every job search needs a home, a place of operation. I had no other alternative but to turn my room into an office, buying file cases, staplers, folders, and markers. I was opening my own company with one objective, to get Micha Berman a job on a cruise ship. I even went so far as to give my company a name, Operation Cruise, Inc. There was only one way to become an expert on the cruise line industry, and that was to read everything published about it. I ordered every possible cruise line publication and had it delivered to my dorm. My mail overflowed with cruise magazines. You name it, I got it, *Cruise Travel Magazine, Ocean and Cruise News, Cruising, Cruise Digest Reports*, among others. Drowning myself in this material I soon learned to speak the language; I could rattle off the names of every single ship in a fleet in one breath as well as the dates new ships were coming out. A transformation had begun.

My dorm room, once sparse and clean became a jungle of boxes, papers, folders, magazines and envelopes. The walls in my room were plastered with large white billboards with inspirational messages on them. My favorite one was from *What Color Is Your Parachute*, a billboard with a hundred "nos" on it and finally one big "yes" at the bottom. Hung above my desk, a poster with a beautiful cruise ship on it and the city of Miami in the background glowed holy light. Another crucial item was my phone and answering machine on which I would leave current news of the cruise line industry on the tape daily, labeling it Mic's Cruise News. During the months I was looking for a cruise job I let everyone I met know I was job searching. I visualized the whole search as a big game, filling my walls with strategy charts and various diagrams tracking my contacts. It was becoming clear that I was creating a war room, heading into uncharted territory and loving the whole experience.

Though I considered my job search a full-time position, I still had college to worry about. I created office hours for myself and fit my class work around my hours of operation. I was running my own class; a mixture of marketing, public speaking, and creative writing. Each morning I woke up and began my workday in my office. At one point, I ran out of space and turned my refrigerator into an extra filing cabinet, an unpopular move with my parents, but providing a uniquely chilled resumé. I quickly discovered that human resources departments in cruise lines were dead ends and were to be avoided at all costs. The question remained, if I were to avoid the human resources department who was I then to contact? The answer was three words: The Entertainment Director.

My mission was now clear. I needed to be within arms length of an Entertainment Director. To make contacts within the cruise lines required major networking and networking was the heart and soul of my entire job search. I intended to connect through several different channels gathering as many contacts as I could through family and friends. Often I wrote congratulation letters to people I had read about in magazines who had been promoted or won awards. However, my largest networking effort was known as Project Random. I wrote to every one of my college and fraternity alumni in the cities of New York, Miami and San Francisco on the whimsical chance that one of these individuals had connections to employees in the cruise lines. Creating a database was so cumbersome, I had to hire another student as an intern. No ordinary letter was sent out. I carefully tailored each letter to alumni; the words emphasized our family bond and the chance of helping a young person early in his career. Sometimes I got lucky and actually found names of alumni who worked directly in the industry. In fact one of the Vice Presidents of a major cruise line was an alumnus and it took one letter and a phone call to set up an interview with the Entertainment Director.

Along with the letters to alumni and Entertainment Directors, I always included my resumé. I figured why not reach out to a wide array of people and get their inside scoops on what made a powerful resumé? One professor suggested I look at magazines and model my resumé with the fashion and style of magazine advertising. At the top of my resumé, like a Broadway marquee, I printed in large boldface: "Conversationalist, Host, Actor, Creative Programmer."

During the time of these mailings I was always on the look out for any type of conventions that featured cruise line representatives. One day I received a flyer in the mail about a Travel Review Conference in Washington D.C.. Cruise line representatives were streaming in to within an hour of where I lived and there was no choice but to be there and meet them. The fee to get into the conference was exorbitant for a frugal college student like myself so I called the organizers and asked if I could volunteer my time to help run the event. A day before the event I showed up at the hotel to stuff gift bags, a requirement for all volunteers. I received the best job, responsibility for the distribution of name tags to attendees of the conference.

Perusing the conference guest list I was delighted to see that the President of The Cruise Line International Association (CLIA), a cruise lobbying group, was to give a speech. I took special care to watch for his arrival since this one man had more than enough contacts to land me jobs in any cruise line out of Miami. After an hour or so most of the name tags were claimed except for his; it seemed I was plain out of luck. Dejected, I began to pack up my belongings and was about to grab some snacks from the courtesy table when down the hall I spied a man in a suit approaching. Could this be my knight in shining armor? He was heading directly for my table. "Hi, I'm Jerome Gottesman. "Jackpot" rang in my mind as I greeted him and gave him his name tag. Too nervous to start any type of conversation, I smiled politely and before I could say a word he was gone. "You stupid idiot, the only reason you're here is to speak to him; now go run after him," I angrily chastised myself. I watched him as he made his rounds, shaking hand after hand. Time was ticking. He broke away from one group and headed to the men's room.

Since this was my only chance to meet him, I darted after Mr. CLIA and approached him, at of all places, the urinal. Of course, I had the courtesy to wait for him to zip up his pants but after that I had no mercy. I gently tapped him on the shoulder. "Um, Hi my name is Micha Berman and I had, I mean, I have been researching the cruise line industry. I am interested in getting a cruise staff position and wanted to ask you for advice." I finally got the words out and now I expected a very polite brush off. Slowly, he turned around. There was a moment of dead silence followed by a gentle smile. "Well hello there. How are you? Great to hear such enthusiasm." He suggested some relevant books, which could aid my search. Needless-to-say, I had already devoured the literature. This man disguised as an angel, disclosed the magical information every job searcher craves, his secretary's name and phone number. "Call anytime," he said. And with those words he hurried out of the bathroom for his speech. I desperately wanted to give him my resumé before he left and then remembered I had brought an article printed in the *Washington Post* the day before about cruising. Sticking two of my resumés in between the rolled up article, I rushed after him. "This will make good reading for the plane ride back," I said. He accepted the newspaper and slipped it into his briefcase. That afternoon all I could do was laugh and think of this man reading my resumé on the plane back to New York. I was truly going nuts!

Then one day it happened. Project Random began to bear fruit as my mailbox overflowed with letters from alumni. On average, I expected to receive over ten pieces of mail each day. Soon it was taking an hour a day just to sort through the mail. Like Charlie breaking open each Wonka chocolate, I hoped and prayed that the letter I was holding in my hands would hold the magic key to the cruise kingdom. My letters had struck a chord and although many alumni admitted they knew no one in the cruise line business, their kindness and support was incredible. Some sent articles, others maps, and some even ripped pages out of their phone books with the numbers and addresses of cruise lines highlighted. I received dinner invitations and several alumni even offered me a place to stay while I was visiting, an offer I would gladly take. Some of the correspondence was very emotional. The mother of one of the alumni wrote in detail how her daughter had died on a street in New York when she was hit by a tractor-trailer. One letter begged me to stay in contact after I got my cruise job—now this was a person who understands the meaning of reverse networking!

Some alumni called me directly. One early morning I woke up to the phone ringing. Half asleep, I mumbled my way through the conversation, took down the name and number and fell back to sleep. Later in the day, I was unable to decipher the phone number but the name was very clear, Dr. Crown. I searched through all the names of the alumni in my computer and finally came up with a match. When I called and spoke with Dr. Crown, his southern accent and soft demeanor intrigued me, but his words seemed peculiar. He invited me to come by his office any time, but wouldn't give me details about any contact he had. I showed up at the address and asked for Dr. Crown's apartment, which also served as his office. As Dr. Crown opened the door a strange odor emanated from the room. It was a stale smell, something old, decaying. Immediately I had images of a serial killer, not an elderly southern gentleman. Dr. Crown could not have been taller than five feet, his old shaggy clothes matching his unshaven face.

"Welcome, come in young man and make yourself comfortable," he said in a creepy tone. I stepped in cautiously to a studio apartment that looked more like a chemistry laboratory. The room was filled with books and as I looked around I saw little furniture and strangely enough no bed. Dr. Crown sat down at a desk and asked me to take a seat. Warning bells went off in my mind but I figured what harm could this little old man do? Apparently, he had been working for over a decade trying to come up with his own cure for AIDS. He was completely committed to the cause, working 12 to 13 hours a day and then pulling out a little foam mattress from his closet to sleep on at night. For what seemed like an eternity he spoke passionately about the AIDS crisis. It seemed fascinating but I didn't see the connection to the cruise line industry. Before I could ask any questions, Dr. Crown began staring at my neck as if he noticed something. "Has anyone ever told you that you might have an enlarged thyroid?" he mentioned casually. "No, not really," I responded. He said he noticed a protrusion from my neck and was curious whether I had certain symptoms of an enlarged thyroid. "Are you tired often?" and "Do you get cold easily?" he asked.

What was really strange was that all the symptoms he had listed I had experienced in the last year. "Would you mind if I feel your thyroid?" he asked. "I guess not," I said before realizing what I was getting into. Dr. Crown slowly rose from his chair and crept behind me. I felt his cold hands wrap around my neck and chills tingled down my spine. I had two thoughts. First, that this man was going to strangle me and I would die in this little decayed studio and end up with my head in a little jar. And second, I thought this man would make a pass at me. I expected a peck, nibble or kiss but nothing happened as he rubbed my neck and said I should probably get it checked out. I needed to get out of the apartment. I quickly explained my search for a cruise job and Dr. Crown responded by saying he was looking for help in his research and thought I might want to earn extra money. Yeah extra money as a love slave, no thanks. "Thank you, Dr. Crown, but I really must be going." As I closed the door behind me I was happy to have escaped. I couldn't help but enjoy the fresh air of the world outside. "No more visits to creepy old alumni," I muttered as I walked back towards campus.

Each day at lunch I tore into the pile of letters waiting for me. I separated the mail into two piles, duds and non-duds. Duds were defined as nice letters but with no real contacts into cruise lines, while non-duds represented the jewels, actual contacts into cruise lines. For the first couple weeks I only received duds but soon my luck turned. The first letter I received in the non-dud category came from a college alumni named Jack who worked for Merrill Lynch in Southern Florida. In the letter he mentioned he had a friend who worked for a cruise line and attached his business card at the bottom edge. Throughout my entire job search I always found it nerve-racking to pick up and call people I did not know. It felt like seventh grade when you had a crush and were terrified to pick up the phone to ask for a date. I dialed the numbers quickly and held the phone to my ear. A man answered and I knew immediately it was Jack. "Well, Micha nice to hear from you," he said. We talked a little but he seemed distracted and distant. I heard kids in the background and realized that this was probably a bad time for him to talk when the conversation turned dramatically. "You know Celebrity Cruises is undergoing some major changes," he said. Did I know, what kind of question was that, after all I had been eating and drinking cruise magazines for months. "Yeah, I know they recently combined with another cruise line," I answered with confidence. "Oh, I see you have been doing your homework; let me make a couple of calls," Jack replied, acknowledging my intensity. Jack's friend would turn out to be the Vice President of Finance for Celebrity Cruise Lines.

My biggest catch of all and one that would eventually land me a job came from a Miami friend named Lisa who I had met several years ago traveling through Europe. Early in my job search I called Lisa to let her know the exciting news that I was probably heading down to Miami to work on a cruise ship. "Oh really, my mother went to high school with the Vice President of one of the large cruise lines down here," she said casually. I could have screamed. Was I hearing this right? I gently prodded not wanting to reveal my excitement about this amazing contact. It turned out her mother was still chummy with the Vice President of Carnival Cruise Lines and went on cruises all the time. A couple of calls later and an interview was set up.

I knew my search was taking off when I received a call from the head of Human Resources at Royal Caribbean begging me to stop doing whatever I was doing. "I don't know what you're doing but I have received seven of your resumés in the past week," he moaned. "That's great," I replied. "No, I don't think you understand, you must stop sending them." He was actually pleading for me to stop! He promised an interview and I promised I would call off the barrage of resumés filling his "in" basket.

After two months of hard work I had gotten commitments from almost all of the major cruise lines for interviews including Costa Cruise Lines, Carnival, Royal Caribbean, Premier Cruise Lines. I started visualizing my trip to Miami. But my frustration had ballooned with Celebrity Cruise Lines where I had been unable to reach the Entertainment Director. Days before I was to leave for Miami I decided to call Jack, my original contact from Merrill Lynch, and asked him to make a few phone calls. He told me he would work on it for me and in less than thirty minutes I received a call in my room from the Entertainment Director herself asking me when I would be available for a meeting. I was in heaven. Miami seemed closer than ever. I bought the ticket, packed my bags, and boarded a plane for the land of beaches and palm trees.

I viewed my trip to Miami as a military operation. Eight interviews in a matter of six days. My plan of attack was quick and precise. I would enter the Entertainment Director's office and in a matter of fifteen minutes convince them I had been preparing for a cruise staff position my whole life. I decided to leave the tanks at home and instead my main source of transport became a Hertz Rent-a-Car. I was fortunate to have a free place to stay thanks to the hospitality of a fraternity alumni. Barry contacted me several weeks before I left for Miami and explained he was a chiropractor who worked close to 70 hours a week. Never at home, he invited me to stay for as long as I desired. When I met him for the first time I have to admit I was a bit worried. After all he was a single man in his fifties. Was he expecting anything from me? Still recovering from Dr. Crown I wondered whether I would end up hanging upside down like a sausage in his closet. After a day or two I couldn't express my appreciation enough for the way he treated me.

I landed in Miami with a secret weapon—preparation. After all I had been studying the cruise line industry for close to a year. As the interviews drew closer I was surprised to feel little nervousness; instead my body was at its bursting point with explosive anticipation. Before my trip I sat for hours thinking of any possible questions I could be asked, scouring every possible job interview book I could get my hands on. I accumulated pages and pages of possible questions and proceeded to answer all of them, covering the spectrum from the simplest, "Why do you want this job," to the more complex, "Tell me a story."

I was to control each interview and if anyone was going to ask questions it should certainly be me. In many ways I was interviewing the cruise lines. I knew I was the right person for the job, but the question remained, was the cruise line right for me? I would come into each office with a prepared speech, always beginning the meeting with a laugh. "It is no accident I am sitting here today," I stated with confidence at the beginning of each interview. I explained the measures I had gone to in researching the job and the industry. I went on "This job is nothing new for me. I have been doing it my whole life." I often compared my dorm to a cruise ship without the water.

I created a folder for each cruise line with articles and facts so I could brief myself before each interview. This allowed me to ask educated questions. I made a point to read a cruise line magazine up to the moment of my interview. I concluded my interviews by presenting the entertainment director with a short pamphlet I had written called "Cruise Creations" which was filled with my ideas for new cruise ship activities. One of my favorites was a movie night in the pool where passengers would lie on rafts and watch "Jaws" on a big screen. I also suggested peanut butter sculpture competitions and honeymoon body painting workshops. I always slyly added, " I'd love to show you more some other time."

Arriving fifteen minutes early at my first interview, I slipped into the bathroom. From my pocket I pulled out my toothbrush and toothpaste. Call it a fixation or obsession but I always liked to know my breath was fresh before I walked into these interviews; it became my little ritual. Sitting in the waiting room I marveled at the showcases with miniature cruise ships. I had finally made it to the offices and in a matter of minutes I would be talking to a real live entertainment director. A young woman stepped out of the hall. "Micha Berman, Miss Young is ready to see you." I slowly followed the secretary down a sunny corridor of offices, every so often peeking in the rooms I was passing to see the palm trees of Miami through the windows. Finally I arrived at a large office and took a step into the room. I was caught off guard by the sight of a stunningly beautiful tanned woman in her forties who greeted me with a firm handshake and offered me a seat. Judging by the absence of any minuscule ounce of body fat on her body, I was sure Miss Young had already lifted weights, swam in the ocean, and sipped her five glasses of orange juice before our meeting. "So you're the one I had to call, huh?" Her voice did not seem pleasant, in fact she seemed angry and resentful. Who was I fooling, she was pissed.

My first interview was getting off to a rocky start. This Entertainment Director, now just a foot away from me, had been forced to call me and set up an interview after I had used my contacts to the Vice President of the company. Unhappy about having to meet me under duress, she bluntly stated her displeasure, which quickly sent me into a panic. "Calm down," I reminded myself as I wiped the cold sweat, which had begun its slow and painful trip down my forehead. My body temperature was on the rise, but my preparation paid off and I was able to eventually slip into my rehearsed routine. I apologized for my aggressive behavior but explained it was the only way to get in the door. "Surely you understand how tough this business is and I did not see any other way of getting a meeting," I pleaded. After a couple more minutes of groveling she began to lighten up and the interview actually began to go quite well. We were getting along and by the time it came to leaving she was smiling and seemed very enthusiastic about my chances. I shook her hand and walked briskly down the corridor and into the elevators. It was done and although it looked shaky at first, I could consider my first interview a success. Except for Royal Caribbean, where my interview was delayed so many times, I ended up sleeping in my car for four hours before I could meet with the Entertainment Director, the interviews went quite well.

My round of interviews were over. I had left a piece of my heart in each office and all that was left was an exhausted soldier. Graduation was approaching and still no word. I kept hearing the question, "Have you got a job yet?" Despite all the complexities of my search, my only answer was "no." I was the superhero of job searches, but what it really came down to was that I had not landed anything yet and it was beginning to look like I might have to turn in my cape. I doggedly tried to follow up with the Entertainment Directors, but no one answered my calls. At times I felt too tired or frustrated to even pick up the phone. To spice up this monotonous task I often made the requisite calls in my underwear while standing on my kitchen table.

Graduation came and went and still no job offer. I began thinking about that machine gun again. I had become a job search zombie hypnotized by rejection. In moments of desperation I thought about actually taking a cruise and cornering the cruise director for a job. Entering my tiny apartment seemed no different that Friday than it had been all year, but as I walked towards my bed the red blinking light of the answering machine caught my attention. I pushed the play button and collapsed on the sofa expecting to hear the usual frustrating hang-ups that so many of my friends had tortured me with over the years. All of a sudden a voice I did not recognize was speaking to me. I listened as the Entertainment Director of Carnival, one of the largest cruise lines in the world, offered me a position. "Please call back as soon as you can," said this stranger who was soon to become my boss. I had landed a dream job. "Oh my God! Oh my God!" I screamed to an empty room as I pounded on the walls. Months and months of frustration washed away as I laughed, yelled, and jumped up and down in my little dorm room. In less than seven days I would board a plane out of Washington D.C. and fly to Miami to join the crew of a 70,000 ton Carnival cruise ship as one of only two Assistant Cruise Directors.

Within days I received offers from Celebrity Cruise Lines and Costa Cruise Lines. As a young single male with an abnormally high hormone level I made an educated decision and went with the "party" cruise line, Carnival. After making my mind up, I had a strange sensation; I was becoming nervous. It was as if I had never accepted the reality of working on a cruise ship. Where would I do my laundry? Would I have my own room? Where would I keep my money? Could I actually live on the ship without puking my brains out? It all seemed too much to handle and the whole affair was beginning to depress me. Would I really be able to handle the pressure of living on a ship? Most of my anxiety came from the simple fact that I had no real idea what a cruise ship looked like and what awaited me. I had prepared as well as I could but unless one has cruised it is impossible to predict what cruise life will be like. The Entertainment Director provided me with few details except my basic salary and to bring white dress pants, a blue blazer and black dress shoes. I imagined arriving at the dock and a man emerging from a compartment of the ship, climbing up a ladder, peeking his head out and motioning me to come in. I later realized I was envisioning a submarine, but this gives an idea of how muddled my state of mind really was during this time.

Finally it was just me, a good friend, Jeff and my family sitting together at the airport terminal waiting for the plane bound for Miami. I was like a little kid going to summer camp, tears streaming down my face. So many emotions and uncertainties overwhelmed me. "Flight 749 to Miami, Florida now boarding," echoed across the airport. There was no turning back. I waved good-bye and walked briskly down the corridor trying to escape the pain of the moment. Wiping the final tears from my eyes, I sat in my seat and looked out the window. Sitting across from me I noticed a young woman who seemed to be experiencing many of my same emotions. Our eyes met and as if I had entered the Twilight Zone, she whispered my name. Tall and slender with dark skin, this woman was a Filipino version of Betty Boop. It turned out she was the new production singer on the same cruise ship I was to work on and had been tipped off by the Entertainment Director that I would be aboard her flight. Lost in conversation, the city of Miami approached quickly. We stepped out to the street, hailed a cab and headed to the hotel the cruise line had set us up with. That evening both of us shared a similar restlessness as we anticipated the excitement of the morning. We stayed up late looking at pictures of our friends and family and ordering room service. I had met my first friend on the cruise ship, Charla. In the morning we were to take our first cruise. Little did I know by the time my cruise adventure would end I would have taken over fifty cruises covering the entire Caribbean, swam with hundreds of stingrays, and kissed passionately under the moonlight.

Crazy Cruise Trivia
Did you know?

Typical food intake on the Explorer of the Seas,
one of Royal Caribbean's largest cruise ships, includes:

Ribs: 1,600 pounds

Chicken: 3,000 pounds

Striploin 2,500 pounds

Shrimp 1,500 pounds

Eggs 40,000

Beer 20,000 cans

Soda 9,000 cans

Liquor 1,000 bottles

Fresh Vegetables 5,000 pounds

Wine 5,000 bottles

Chapter 2
Love at First Sight

I was off to meet the cruise ship. This was a blind date I would never forget and one I could never really prepare for. Driving through the port that morning I fixated on the fleet of cruise ships, each shining in the sun with their unique multicolored logo. My heartbeat quickened with the sighting of each new vessel, each one signaling that my destiny was drawing closer. The ships were beasts, larger than anything I had seen before, draped by collections of bright colors exploding off their hulls like a trapeze artist. Before long I would be able to identify all of these ships merely by their signature contours from as far as a half mile away, but for now they were strangers, new and unfamiliar. The parking area in front of the fleet of cruise liners was a colony of bustling humanity, passengers moving in patterns of ants, some going up escalators with their baggage, others running after personnel, and many hugging and driving off in a puff. Some travelers had already starting gathering on the decks of the ships preparing for the famous "bon voyage," waving to the unfortunate who would remain on land. It was a cornucopia of noise, commotion and emotion. This was the front yard of my new home. Arriving at the proper gate I blinked in disbelief for this ship was even bigger than the others. I had finally arrived at my destination, Carnival Cruise Line's M.S. Ecstasy. I stood frozen, my eyes exploring every inch of this mammoth, my neck straining as I gazed straight up as I would to see the top of a skyscraper. The other ships in the harbor were sail boats compared to this cruise ship, which stood 13 stories high and looked more like an office building than a sea vessel. I looked back at the cab driver and in elated shock whispered to no one in particular "this thing is a whale, a big white whale." Its employees alone numbered over 800 and including passengers, this ship was a small floating city housing over 2900 people.

I sneaked myself into the busy passenger terminal, up an elevator, down a narrow walkway and found myself standing at the center called the Atrium on the Empress Level of the bustling cruise ship. And again I was held in its mesmerizing grip. All I could see were walls of glass and bright neon lights enveloping me. My body was brimming with anticipation as I kept thinking, "this place is amazing." Long lines had already begun to form at the information desk where I could see young people in crisp white uniforms handing out keys to the anxious and excited vacationers. I could have been in the middle of a suburban shopping mall, luxury was not a prevailing mood, but rather a subdued tackiness. Several drab sofas filled the corners of the atrium with blaring television sets placed symmetrically between them, perched up high like in a hospital room. Glass elevators whizzed up and down transporting passengers to the pool area on the Lido deck. To describe the scene as futuristic would be an injustice to aliens of another species, rather it was mini-Vegas at sea with a dash of Willie Wonka thrown in.

I was shown to the cruise director's office and greeted there by a man younger than I expected, who shook my hand and welcomed me in his clipped British accent. "We've been waiting for you," Gary said with a friendly smile. On the floor sat a pretty young woman in her early 20s named Sam, the other assistant cruise director. The cabin, spacious in design, appeared no different than a one-bedroom apartment, its shelves overflowed with liquor and bootleg videos. Gary had been on the ship for a while and had set up for himself a very cozy home with none of the glitter in the façade of the boat. Having begun as a bartender, Gary had worked his way up to one of the most desirable positions on the ship. He appeared friendly, charming, witty, supremely confident and a bit on the round side. His belly was hard to ignore, it had a life of its own sitting there, bouncing, and entertaining me with its somersaults and awkward motions. I could tell it was an old friend by the way Gary carried himself.

All first timers on a cruise ship, or sea virgins as Gary liked to joke, go through an initiation phase, replete with good natured hazing and harmless ribbing about life on the ship. "Don't worry mate, you'll know this ship like the back of your hand," Gary assured me in a tone of devilish delight. I received a schedule of activities for the week and was told to be backstage for an introduction show at 10:30 p.m.. I quickly glanced at the schedule but was too fired up to actually focus on the information.

I hurriedly left his cabin, eager to discover my new home. Wandering aimlessly around the ship, I was amazed at the sheer number of rooms and corridors. There seemed to be endless hallways with tacky blue carpeting as far as I could see as I traveled the length of the ship. Each turn greeted me with another sign and an arrow pointing to the disco or the swimming pool, the jacuzzi, or the day care center, the library, or the skeet shooting gallery. This ship had everything! Abruptly, the horn blew, signifying the ship was about to leave. It was a sound I had heard so many times on the *Love Boat*, and now it meant one thing—life was about to change and anyone you saw around you now was aboard for the adventure.

I scurried to the top of the ship to join the passengers. It was a rare place, so much happiness in such a confined area. Everybody was hugging, jumping up and down, laughing and waving to the crowds down below on the dock and yes, there was even confetti. The hubbub became louder and louder as the ocean liner inched away from the pier. In many ways I shared their uncontrolled elation as I looked out at the beautiful image of Miami fading away. As we passed fellow cruise ships Gary made wise cracks about all the other cruise lines like, "Hello everybody aboard Royal Caribbean's Sovereign of the Seas, sorry to hear you will have no alcohol this week, but enjoy your cruise!" Soon we were surrounded by ocean. The passengers quickly dispersed in all directions to explore the ship, but I remained rooted to my spot, contemplating the scene around me. I was not a passenger and yet I was a traveler and a visitor on this cruise liner, anxious to find its rhythms and ways. I didn't fully understand my role yet but as I looked out at the sparkling blue ocean and felt the frothy waves crashing up against the hull, my body was filled with euphoria. Happy and content, I inhaled the crisp sea air and thought about all the people who mattered to me back home. I reflected on the trip I was about to undertake. There is something about looking out at the ocean that makes people do a lot of thinking and I was no exception. Was I making the right decision? Would I last? Taking one last glimpse at the water I turned and headed back to my cabin.

Since I had a couple of hours before the introduction show, I decided to go back to my room and unpack. After walking through the passenger areas all day long, my curiosity for the crew areas had grown. Below the main level of the ship existed a world unto itself, the decks where the hundreds of crew members worked and lived. As I walked through these decks it dawned on me that I was entering a different neighborhood, one with its own culture and rarely seen by passengers. The first sign that you had entered crew city was the obvious lack of carpeting on the floors and the sheer bareness of the shiny metal walls. The exuberant colors of the passenger halls were replaced by a stark hospital like setting and a general feeling of unadorned survival. A second clue that this was not passenger living quarters was the trash littering the floors, the most common item a shred of wet cardboard standing guard outside a crew member's door, the last remnant from a six pack of beer. Finally in this new neighborhood, hallways also served as soccer fields. Crew members, many from Latin America, often held soccer matches in these hallways not wider than 3 feet, during their off hours, bouncing off the doors, screaming and hollering, there was no way to stop them from enjoying their national pastime.

The staff living quarters consisted of five decks. The lower the floor, the more cramped and dirty the conditions and the more unsafe it was to wander. Think of it as the United Nations with the top floors representing the rich and fortunate nations of the world like the United States, Europe and oil rich countries like Saudi Arabia and the United Arab Emirates. The bottom floors might be closer to third world countries such as India, Sudan, or Guatemala. Fortunately, my room was on the highest level, an area reserved for managers and special guests. Whereas each deck below had cabins with bunk beds for two crew members and sometimes an extra cot for three people, my floor had all singles, many of them with portholes.

It was the cleanest crew deck with the most services available. However, on one of the largest cruise ships in the world, the rooms still seemed tiny. As I stepped into my cabin, I couldn't help thinking I was moving into an office cubicle, one with dimensions no larger than nine feet by nine feet. This room made my college dorm seem like a Ritz Carlton Suite. If I stood in the middle of the room with my arms fully outstretched,

I came pretty close to touching the walls. The walls, bare except for a couple of minor holes where thumbtacks once stood, were painted a dull tan color punctuated by tiny metal reminders such as "no smoking in cabin," or "life vest available under bed." The total inventory of furniture was minimal, a small desk, cabinet armoire, the style akin to ones at a clearance sale from a furniture wholesale dealer somewhere in Brooklyn. A phone hung on the wall that connected to all crew members' rooms, but not to passenger cabins.

I stepped through the narrow door leading to the bathroom where I confirmed once again that just stretching my arms out would allow me to touch the sink, toilet and shower simultaneously. This opened up the possibility of showering and peeing into the toilet at the same time, a male feat worth bragging about. I felt lonely staring at this sterile room, its lack of permanence bringing my spirits down like a depressant. In a couple months I transformed the room into a much cozier place as I shipped in my television, VCR, CD player and computer. There was no reason for all my goodies to be locked up in storage; this was my new home and I wanted it to feel like it. The most disheartening feature about my first room was the lack of a port hole, the mariner's version of a window. When I woke up every morning it was pitch black and I had no idea whether it was noon or ten in the evening, let alone what the weather was like. I felt like I was in some *National Geographic* science experiment, the ones where people are secluded in subterranean caves and not allowed to know the time of day. Eventually, I was moved to a cabin with a port hole and it literally lit up my day to be able to see the sunshine in the morning.

The intercom clicked on. "May I have your attention please, this is your Captain speaking. In approximately 15 minutes we will be having a boat drill. We ask that all passengers and crew report to their assigned stations." The words were spoken in a thick Italian accent, every three words grouped together in illogical islands of grammar. My job was to stand at the top of a stairwell on deck and instruct the yawning passengers where to go. They were supposed to have their life jackets already on, but in most cases the only thing they were thinking about was whether to have their margaritas salted or not.

The boat drill was supposed to be simple, as passengers only had to take a glimpse at the life vests in their cabin to discover where to go; it was all wonderfully color coded. However cruise goers were too overwhelmed by the ship to think about anything practical during their first hour at sea except to marvel at the size of the ship and the fun and games to come. After twenty minutes the drill was declared over by the Captain. His deep lilting voice was heard throughout the ship as he thanked the passengers for their cooperation and wished everyone a great vacation.

Exhausted, I returned to my cabin for a nap. The Introduction Show would begin in two hours. My eyelids heavy like sandbags, I sunk gracefully into bed. Oversleeping the buzz of my alarm clock, I quickly rushed to get my navy blue pants and blazer on. My heart beat a rapid dance as I realized I would be late to my first event on the ship. This was the last thing I needed on top of my anxiety over my first public appearance as Assistant Cruise Director. I was close to a nervous wreck as I sprinted down the hall to reach the Sapphire Lounge, a large theatre seating over 1500 people. Arriving backstage just in time I could hear Gary's unique voice warming up the audience with corny jokes. The passengers loved Gary and his carefully suited blend of sardonic and self-effacing sick British style of humor that many Americans don't quite get. Since my father hailed from South Africa, once a part of the British Commonwealth, I was well-trained in this type of good natured humor and quite at home in its wickedness.

The Introduction Show was the big event on the first evening of the cruise and it was literally the only show in town. Passengers filled the Sapphire Lounge to meet their cruise director and the rest of staff who will entertain them throughout the week. I had already met most of the dancers who made up the entertainment cruise staff and frankly there was no better way to describe them than gifts from God. I considered myself a pretty decent looking guy, six feet tall, brown curly hair with turtle green eyes, but these women were stunning. British and beautiful, the curvaceous dancers were always fun to be around. They were incredibly open and acted with few inhibitions, unlike any American their age I had ever met. Like their ring leader Gary, they were loud, crude and provocative, a combination I really enjoyed. Samantha was a gorgeous buxom blonde with a body that created traffic jams on the ship. Her penchant for pulling up her top at the most opportune moments created an enormous fan club; behind the façade Samantha was a sincere gal with a sharp mind to go with the killer body. Tracy, a brunette with eyes as innocent as the ocean and a giggle as precious as a teddy bear, was looking for that special someone, and was often lost in thought about her family and life back in England. Paula, a statuesque and slender aerobics instructor turned dancer was one of those rough blue collar types with a low voice and a tough demeanor to boot. It was hard to tell whether she wanted to love you or beat you. Claire, petite and cute as can be, was the thespian in the group, dramatic and when not reciting Shakespeare, reciting the list of ex-boyfriends she left behind in London. To complement this team of gorgeous amazons was Simon and Richard, two gay male dancers. Simon, tall and lanky, Richard, short and stocky, queens by nature and as proud and vituperative as I had ever met. This was the staff I was to live and work with.

I would eventually work backstage with the dancers and got used to them walking naked in front of me. For most males backstage, meaning Richard and Simon, this was not an issue; for me it was a fringe benefit of the job. Many times during the evening performances I would catch a stagehand peering into the women's dressing room which explained why many a night the timing of show's cues were just a bit off. Over the next few months I would develop little crushes on certain dancers but they never seemed to match the intensity of the dancers that became enamored with me. Many of them had studied dance in England and this was their first professional job. We all gathered behind the heavy red curtain where we heard the cruise director beginning his welcome speech to the captivated audience. Each week Gary would run through the same jokes and each week the audience would go crazy with laughter. "The buffets are so good here, you come on as passengers and we ship you off as cargo." At a certain moment in his speech he would mention the cruise staff and that was a signal for us to come out. We would march on stage and introduce ourselves one by one. Each British dancer would reveal the town they were from in England, "Cotswald, Shrewsbury, Stratford, and York." Some weeks Richard would proudly yell his hometown as loud as he could. It meant absolutely nothing to the American audiences who looked befuddled and confused by the strange accent and even stranger town names. Finally my turn would come and I would say that I was from the United States and the place would go nuts with applause. Next I would say Washington D.C., the closest relative to my actual hometown of Baltimore, Maryland and the arena roared like I had just declared my intention to run for President. I felt patriotic every time I stood up there as the sole American on staff. It was the Olympics every Sunday night and I had the gold medal clinched.

After introductions Sam and I would remain on stage with Gary. It was time for a game called spoons. Sam and I walked out into the audience and picked out six people to bring them up on stage. Certain passengers were dying to come up, but I often picked on the ones trying to pretend they were invisible. It was sort of cruel but there was always a gem living inside one of those shy bodies. I lined my team up alternating men and women. The cruise director would show two spoons each with a long string attached to the audience and instruct that the first team to take the spoon through each team member's shirt and pants from one end of the team to the other would be the winners. Gary would instruct us to pick women with low cut dresses or exposed cleavage in order to create excitement. It was all orchestrated down to a tee. It was part game show, part televangelist revival. The crowd roared with laughter as the spoon was pulled through each member's clothes. Often the spoon would get stuck in one of the passenger's undergarments, including one night when we had to perform an emergency operation and cut the string. "You all just wish you were the spoon," Gary would predictably joke. As Gary stood next to the winners I would bend the spoon behind my back and then hand it over to him. He would show the bent spoon and give a crazy look to the last member of the team. Guffaws and laughs would erupt from all sides of the theatre.

After handing out champagne to all the participants, Gary wished everyone a good night and the first evening came to a close. Passengers went on their way to explore the ship or get an early night sleep for the next day. It had merely been one day, simply eight hours but in ship time and for everything I had seen and experienced on my first day on the M.S. Ecstasy, I had lived a lifetime. Though my mind was eager to find all the hidden treasures awaiting me on the ship, I was drained and the only place I could dream of was that small prison-like cabin I called home. Soon I was still, breathing evenly while rocking to sleep in the giant arms of my aquatic mother and new friend, the white whale that had so intimidated me at first was slowly becoming familiar.

Crazy Cruise Trivia
Did you know?

Dramamine has not always been
the recommended cure for seasickness or "mal de mer."
Some interesting favorites of the past two centuries include:

Tomato sauce

Pork Fried with Garlic

Cocaine

Morphine

Sea Root

Arrowroot with wine

Sea Water

Mustard Leaf

Chapter 3
Man on the Mike

Any loyal fan of the *Love Boat* knows that every cruise began with a shot of Julie McCoy standing on the gangway, wearing an infectious smile, greeting arthritic travelers in her perfectly tailored uniform while clutching a small brown clipboard close to her heart. True to television, my job as Assistant Cruise Director was first to smile as much as humanly possible and second to guard with my life that magical clipboard containing the endless array of games, contests, and tournaments that would entertain each and every Carnival customer. Each morning a newsletter with the activities for the day, including trivia contests, bingo and shuffleboard information, would be slipped under vacationers' cabin doors. My job was to facilitate all of these games and provide the running commentary; my nickname could have been the "man on the mike." Whenever any type of event required an announcer or "M.C.," I was called upon. Most people freeze with a microphone in their face, but since grade school I had been faking a microphone with my thumb and a clenched fist, announcing confidently to my loyal gang of childhood chums, "Welcome to the Micha Berman Show." I had graduated to prime time and now my voice was booming to audiences from all over America, well kind of. I wasn't exactly Dick Clark, but rather his three-eared demented cousin who had been locked up in the attic for too long performing to a captive audience.

Cruise activities are a form of extreme sports for the recently inebriated. Among our zaniest selection was the ping-pong stuffing competition for newlywed couples. This event took place on the Lido deck that contained all the pools on the ship as well as a pair of jacuzzis. During the day this part of the ship was crowded with sunbathers lying on those cheap greenish blue lounge chairs that populate every community pool in America and freeze in the most unfortunate poses. For the truly risqué, an upper level on the Lido served the topless crowd and soon became a favorite sightseeing destination for curious peeping toms and male crew members. The Lido flowed with music and reeked of grease as a reggae band played all day long surrounded by buffets of endless fatty assortments of hamburgers, hot dogs and french fries. Each corner of this entertainment center was bookmarked by a huge bar with ten foot mirrors and racks of liquor bottles serviced by an army of bar waiters. Tray upon tray of rainbow concoctions were delivered to the kings and queens in their greenish thrones while little children played at their feet.

After the reggae band finished their first set, Harold, the lead singer, would wink at me, my cue to enter and take over the entertainment. I climbed to the edge of the pool with my microphone in hand and spoke the magic words, " I am looking for a few honeymoon couples who are looking to have some fun, come on up!" The couples would jump into the pool and fill their partners bathing suit with as many ping pong balls as they could in 60 seconds. The couple that stuffed the most balls was declared the winner and it was my job to make jokes along the way and make sure the ping pong balls remained white after the games were over (one of my sick jokes). On good days I followed this event with a belly flop contest tempting the tipsy tourists to challenge the waters of the pool with their pink fleshy stomachs—the pool won every time.

Then there was the beer drinking competition, an event most passengers had been training for all week anyway. Americans are tremendous beer drinkers, but no one did it better than the Germans. I started the competition by grouping passengers into fours and the first person to down a can of beer and turn it upside on their head moved into the next round of competition. Finally, in the end, we were left with two coed teams who competed against each other to see who could drink a yard of beer (equivalent of 3 to 4 beers) first. I witnessed incredible drinking feats during my time on the ship including one couple that appeared to have been trained in Germany's Black Forest beer drinking academy, finishing the yard of beer in an incredible eight seconds. The woman who I will always think of as a Helga, consumed most of the spirit. Often, if passengers didn't vomit from seasickness, the beer drinking competition did the trick.

All of the events of the week built up to the finale on the last night of the cruise with the Male Lingerie Competition. Each week over fifty men fought for the right to be named Queen of the Cruise Ship. Why would fathers, doctors, plumbers, businessmen from states as diverse as Texas, Alabama and Florida all fight for the chance to dress up as a woman and parade in front of their 2000 fellow cruisers is a mystery I never could figure out. It was the closest thing to the World Wide Wrestling Federation that ever possessed our ship. An hour before the event I would gather all the contestants in a lounge to go over the rules and hand out an information sheet prying for such vital information as chest size, favorite position and secret fantasy. Each man was adorned with a wig and wore the ugliest dress or undergarments their wives and girlfriends could salvage from their suitcases. Pink was a popular color to go with the dark pulsating lipstick stamped on their face. The scene each week in the lounge was absurd as the guys chased each other around the room trying to squeeze their recently constructed breasts. Stodgy forty-year-olds became a pack of screaming teenage lunatics in a matter of seconds with me as their babysitter.

Of all the weekly activities, Gary hated this one with a passion. Each week he would beg me to do the event for him but would eventually give in minutes before he was to go on. As Gary introduced them on stage to a roaring audience of family and traumatized friends, he read their name, measurements, and secret fantasies with a playful melody in his voice. Names such as Delicious Debbie, Tanky Tommy, Hot Lips Harry, and Booby Bobby set the tone for an adult-themed event. Despite his dislike for the show, Gorgeous Gary knew how to pull it off and by the end of the evening the amused audience was giving him a standing ovation. I set up certain contestants beforehand to say a certain line or try to pinch Gary on the butt, not that they needed too much prodding. Finally, when a winner had been chosen Gary would catch the New Queen of the Ecstasy off guard, dipping them making it look as if he was kissing him. Each evening had its share of exhibitionism as certain passengers had a hard time keeping certain parts inside their lingerie. It was a sausage factory gone wrong.

Eventually Carnival canceled this event due to a small but vocal contingent that complained of unacceptable lewdness, an apt description. Frankly, I was surprised it lasted as long as it did.

Game shows are often criticized for being staged, pre-arranged or just downright scams. Gary was the pope of deception, the world's best malevolent con artist dressed in a cruise director's suit. Each week a newlywed game was played between three couples. Gary always picked two young couples and one elderly couple. He would prepare the game so on the last question in a nostalgic nod to the Chuck Eubank's Newlywed Game of the 1970's, he would ask, "Where was the last place you made whoopee?," The elderly couple replied without hesitation, "the shower on the cruise ship." The crowd roared with laughter and cheers every single week. He would talk to the participants on stage whispering answers without the crowd noticing his actions. Gary had a tremendous talent for making it seem as if the passengers were winning unbelievable prizes. In most cases, the prizes were cheap plastic trophies in the shape of a cruise ship that fell apart in a matter of days, keeping me busy on Sundays as I glued them together and salvaged them for another Newlywed Game.

In addition to leading activities I gave tour talks that on the surface were supposed to be about all the cool places tourists could see while exploring the islands. However, Gary cleverly crafted these talks into large hypnosis sessions, convincing every passenger to visit all the specifically Carnival-approved shops and buy and then buy and then buy a little more. Questions were often the same. "Where do you go to shop for the best gold?" or "Where do you find great pearls?" I knew nothing of jewelry and mostly deferred to Gary, who also knew even less, but spoke effortlessly on where to buy the best silver or pearls on this continent or where to find his friend Harry who would give you a special "cruise ship" price. Part of Gary's salary was directly tied to the sales totals so he had great incentive to lead his little mice to the right destinations and week after week the Pied Piper never failed. For several years, Gary led the Carnival fleet in sales as witnessed by his large collection of expensive watches and jewelry displayed on his wrist, all gifts from the same stores he hustled during his talks.

Gary wasn't against using his tricky talents of persuasion on staff either. Cruise directors compare to American Presidents or Hollywood stars when it comes to public visibility on a cruise ship. It was impossible for him to walk a hundred yards without being swarmed by cruisers who recognized him from the stage. Like a species from Darwin's writings, Gary developed a survival skill, the ability to rid people from his presence, a talent he shared with a skunk, except he sprayed his victims with words. This often meant outright lying or pointing people in the wrong direction. He was a master of deception and to this day I can't help but think this British fellow would make an ideal American politician.

Our ship sailed for six days before returning to Miami on Sunday to prepare for a new cruise. Every other Sunday I would work in the office welcoming fresh new crew members aboard while reordering supplies or any other paperwork that needed to be completed, as well as gluing together the infamous plastic trophies. The most popular item on the ship for crew members was the red polo cruise staff shirt. Two crew members who were getting off the ship stopped by my office saying that Gary had called me and requested that they get two of these shirts. I knew we had been out of these shirts for weeks but was intrigued to hear the Carnival employees tell the story of how they had just witnessed Gary pick up the phone and call me to confirm that there were T-shirts available. With no limits to Gary's shenanigans, he had faked the phone conversation, just another one of his scams. Despite Gary's antics, I really had nothing to complain about. He manipulated me minimally and always with my knowledge for I had seen his game too closely and was a willing accomplice.

The events on the ship run by Gary and his cruise staff provided many laughs; however, much of entertainment on the ship was done by performers who didn't live on the Ecstasy. These were the "fly-on," entertainers that included jugglers, magicians, comedians and singers from all over the country. They were flown to certain ports and then tendered to the ship in order to perform the evening act. Many of these performers could have easily fit into Barnum & Bailey's line up including a French juggler who only used his legs, a Bulgarian couple who twisted themselves into more variations than pretzels and an Australian man who claimed to be the strongest human being on earth. I couldn't argue with him after he balanced himself on his pinkie. At first they seemed like freaks of nature but each performer had a story to tell and as the assistant cruise director it was my job to welcome them each week onto the ship, set them up in a room and make sure they had everything they needed. Their actual performance time often lasted less than 10 minutes and within hours they were off the ship and only seen again several weeks later. They soon became friends and people I looked forward to seeing and I soon realized that by avoiding living on the ship they held on to a bit more sanity than many of my shipmates.

One evening I found myself in the Moonlight Lounge at the back of the ship for a late show featuring a new comedian and a fly-on act. Often I prepped myself before the show studying their past performances and bios and for most of the fly-ons I knew them like they were my neighbor. As usual, I began my remarks talking about all the previous places he had performed when slowly I came to a scary realization that I had no idea what his name was and I was seconds away from a major faux pas. My nervousness grew as I babbled on about playing in Fort Lauderdale and the Improv in New York, hoping for a divine intervention. Unable to wait any longer, I pulled the microphone as close to my mouth as possible, and mumbled, " Would you please welcome to the stage 'RRRHTTTRRRR,'" and ran off the stage. My humiliation was confirmed when I saw Gary sitting at the back bar having a drink and laughing. He told me later he knew a few seconds into my opening that I was in trouble and that I had forgotten the comedian's name; I had a crazy look on my face like I was lost or peeing in my pants or both. From then on, I made a point to learn the performer's name well in advance of the show. There were to be no more mistakes.

My announcing skills also brought me into close contact with the top officers of the ship. Every once in a while I was asked to make an announcement to the whole ship from the bridge since the Italian officers were embarrassed about their poor English skills. By law the officers on the bridge, the area where the ship was actually steered, had to make announcements on safety several times during the cruise. They had a large book filled with hundreds of pages covered by tattered plastic containing every code and instruction on fire safety, life boat procedure, time change notes, weather warning—it was all in there.

The first time I found my way up there I was terrified, expecting to have a captain with a black eye patch bark orders at me and treat me with disdain. Instead I found all of the equipment of the bridge with its many buttons, knobs, maps, flashing lights quite intimidating, but the Captain and Staff Captain turned out to be genteel older fellows who actually offered me a glass of Chianti. I kept looking for a steering wheel dumbfounded by how two men steered a 70,000 ton ship through the seas and maneuvered the beast into the narrow ports. It was quite a testament to their skill and an awful lot of responsibility on their shoulders, which I would find out they were well compensated for. "How do you pronounce that word," Captain Gallo asked me as he pointed to the large book opened on the table. Their English level matched that of a Maitre D' at a local Italian restaurant in the mall, heavily slurring words butchered like wounded soldiers, yet both men stood proud and continued to talk despite their struggle with the language. Captain Gallo, a stout olive skinned man in his late forties who probably stood less than five foot four, despite his dashing good looks and suave demeanor simply could not put an English sentence together without causing havoc. This leader of the ship, ruler of the cruise liner universe pleaded with me like a child to read the full message on the intercom so that everyone would understand, and more importantly he wouldn't break into a cold sweat and have to suffer through a reading. "Please, just this time," he urged as he nudged me closer to the microphone. I made a commitment to tutor Captain Gallo and did my best to spend any free time I had in the bridge improving his speaking skills, offering new vocabulary and building his confidence so one day he would step up to the microphone without fear and chant a flawless public announcement.

Over time I learned more and more about Captain Gallo and slowly but surely his English improved. As a confidant of the Captain and protected under the auspices of King Gary, my life on the ship was cushy at best and privileged at worst. Everyone left me alone to do my job and as the weeks passed, I was amazed at the few hours I had to actually work. I showed up for my two activities per day, but was allowed to have leisure time similar to everyone else vacationing on the ship. When not working I did not have to wear a uniform and could enjoy the ship without being recognized as staff. I received a paycheck each week, money that seemed undeserving. Best of all I had little supervision under Gary who was too busy having a good time to monitor my whereabouts. As long as there were no major crises, Gary remained happy and rarely checked up on me. For the moment life was sweet.

During the first couple of months on the ship, every friend and relative I talked to on the phone wanted to taste this good life. Somewhere in our phone conversations there would be a slight hesitation and I could just predict the question about to come out of their mouths. "Hey man, can you get me a job on the ship?" or "Can you hook me up?" were the bluntest forms of inquiry followed by more subtle, "It must be fun out there, any chance you can find something for your Aunt Perle?" Everyone on land wants to be adrift at sea and many at sea, dream of being on land. It was the aquatic Murphy's law. I had to let these dreamers down gently but the truth was life at sea was not easy; in fact, the reality of working on a cruise ship was far from the fantasy that everyone creates in their minds. Most positions on a cruise ship were completely undesirable; in fact, they made Cinderella's job description look promising.

Work was both tedious and time consuming. Lauren, a friend of mine from Trinidad, lived the typical cruise life, he vacuumed the same section of the ship each and every morning. By the time I was heading to sleep eleven or twelve hours later, I would still see him vacuuming the carpets. Lauren didn't speak English very well, but he always anxiously awaited conversation. We would talk about his family, gossip about the ship, but sometimes during the conversation his face would light up with a smile and he would ask me if I had any luck with the ladies. After a while I figured out what he was thinking about all those hours vacuuming. My position was the cream of the crop. Whereas, I had all the time in the world to enjoy the ports, most workers like Lauren were busy on the ship during these hours performing menial labor. Their lives were all work and little play.

Lauren was lucky to get off the ship once a month; yet his time away was limited and he was only allowed about five hours off from his duties. The hours of my job depended heavily on whether the ship was at sea or docked at port. However, most employees continued to work, regardless of the location of the ship. Even in port the beds still had to be made and the hallways vacuumed. Once passengers left the ship I had all the free time in the world. I was allowed to go anywhere on the ship, but most staff were not permitted to be in passenger areas except when they were directly working there. Lauren worked his eleven to twelve hours and then immediately returned to the crew area.

It is not surprising that few Americans are hired on these cruise ships. My guess is most would get off the ship after the first week. Many of the ship's employees were from the third world, largely Asia, Latin

American and the Caribbean. Countries like India, El Salvador, Thailand, Jamaica led the parade of nations on the crew decks. These working conditions were familiar to them and in certain situations, life on this ship was more promising than their country of origin. Foreign workers felt powerless; sometimes their round trip tickets were held hostage by the cruise authorities in order to force them to stay longer. When I had been offered the job I bought my own ticket, an action that later on I would be very grateful for. For now I wasn't really thinking about returning home, I was enjoying my freedom, my rounds of golf on Caribbean courses, my free time watching movies, reading books and soaking in the sun.

Yes, it was true I had to smile a lot and wear a uniform almost as tacky as Julie McCoy and yes, I had to inhale the pungent smell of beer as it streamed down peoples faces in the beer drinking competition and bounced its stinging way to my eyes. And stroking men's hairy chests in the weekly "Hairy Chest Competition" was not something my parents had aspired for me. Listening to Gary's repeated dialogue and shameless shenanigans was tiresome, but in the end I had a dream job, one that many coveted and one that really felt like a vacation. As long as I had the magical clipboard and microphone in my hand, life in the spotlight wasn't so bad. All I had to do was watch my fellow employees and realize I was a fortunate fellow.

Crazy Cruise Trivia
Did you know?

A ship's registry tells little about it including where it is from. Often cruise ships have "flags of convenience" which means the ship's registry is a country with minimal or no taxes such as Liberia, Panama, Bahamas, Cyprus and Honduras:

Chapter 4
Separate Lives

Getting ready to go to bed one night, I had a strange feeling that the cruise ship had come to a complete stop, and an eerie silence hung over every corner of my cabin. Sleeping on a ship I had grown accustomed to the rhythmic sounds of the motors and engines, singing me to sleep each night like a mother's sweet lullaby. I was puzzled by the absence of song and knew something had happened or in the vernacular of the seas, "something had gone down." I picked up the phone and called Johnny. "What's going on dude?"

"Check this out," he answered, bursting to reveal some kept secret. "A brawl broke out in the crew kitchen and some guy poured a pot of boiling water over some other guy's head." I knew tension existed between crew members but this sounded a bit bizarre. "Yeah, Tracy saw the guy on the way to the infirmary, he was in fetal position screaming at the top of his lungs." His tone swayed between fascination and utter disgust, the way someone might describe meeting a two-headed cat or some other anomaly of nature. Rumor had it that these two crew members had been lovers, pure speculation but the *National Enquirer* hot gossip sold well on the ship and was a convenient antidote to boredom. Any tabloid could have set up shop on our ship, gossip was an appendage on every crew member's sleeve. I had heard of some pretty crazy rumors — cut off penises, people thrown overboard, and love triangles turned bloody, but this was the first event I had witnessed up close and personal. Gay lovers, jealousy, hot water, and a cruise ship – it had all the ingredients of a raunchy novel or an Geraldo episode. The ship was close enough out of our last port that the Captain had decided to turn around and head back for emergency services.

The kitchen staff involved in this fiasco were only two out of 800 employees aboard our cruise ship, all organized in different departments recognizable by their uniforms. One of the groups I had already become familiar with were the officers of the ship, the royalty on this city at sea. The officers on the M.S. Ecstasy, like Captain Gallo, were all Italian and could be spotted instantly by their sparkling clean white uniforms juxtaposed with their dark Mediterranean skin and god-like good looks. Their responsibility was singular and unmatched, simply the awesome task of running the mechanics of a 70,000 ton ship and safeguarding the lives of over 2900 people. The top echelon of the officers club consisted of the Captain and his second in command, the Staff Captain. Captain Gallo, by now an English student of mine, was deeply respected by the crew and fawned upon by passengers who circled his presence in rock star fashion.

As chief disciplinarian on the ship, or sea sheriff, as cruise staff liked to call him, Captain Gallo had the power to arrest anyone at any time and throw them into jail or the brig. The brig, located down on the corridor from where the dancers lived, was a continual site of fascination for crew members. Although at first glance the plain metal door blended seamlessly into the regular pattern of the hallway, a closer furtive look into the scratched circular window revealed a cramped cell complete with prison bars, a bare bed and a stiff metal chair.

One evening while heading back to my cabin, I heard loud desperate shrieking. "Help, get your fucking hands off me; let me go!!" As I turned the hall I saw two security guards dragging a portly man by his arms while his feet combed the carpet behind him, his eyes bulging out of his head in a devilish stare. On a whim, this passenger experimented with cocaine in his cabin and was becoming a real disruption to the midnight buffets, a sin punishable by death on a pleasure boat like the Ecstasy. The guards led him to the brig for a good night sleep; however, sleep wasn't on his agenda. His drug-induced pleas and moans echoed throughout the night and finally ended the next morning when he was taken off the ship and handed over to local police, which in the case of Jamaica or Mexico meant his cruise was officially over.

The security guards, mostly of Indian descent with English skills that made Captain Gallo look like an English professor, were not intimidating; in fact, they often reminded me of rent-a-cops hired for parties. Standing in hallways around the ship they stared vacuously, often using their disciplinary powers on young children running through the halls of the ship or assisting seniors up the steps. The rate of turnover for these protectors was constant. I came to believe that most of them didn't even recognize me as an Assistant Cruise Director, allowing me free rein to violate rules right in front of their faces with impunity.

The Captain of the ship determined how strict ship rules would be enforced or in many cases, not enforced. In fact, the mood of the ship for staff was directly a reflection of who was captain at the time. One dictatorial captain who followed Captain Gallo posted flyers on the walls whenever a crew member was caught breaking a rule, detailing who the person was and what offense they committed—maybe a reincarnation of a colonial governor from the day of the Puritans. One cabin steward was guilty of public drunkenness, another waiter was publicly castigated for missing curfew, each of their shave-deprived faces appeared on signs resembling FBI Most Wanted posters. It was a step back into the middle ages and I often expected to witness public spankings on the Lido deck, maybe with some upbeat music from the reggae band as the fitting anachronistic accompaniment. Another captain threw a staff party every month, providing beer and endless amounts of food in an orgy of late night entertainment. Captain Gallo was somewhere in between, enforcing the major rules, providing order but also maintaining an air of compassion and desire to see the crew happy and motivated.

By far the officers are the best paid employees on the ship with the captain and staff captain's salaries in the six digits. One staff captain talked of his upcoming vacation and admitted he just didn't know what to do anymore, what with several months of vacation each year and the constant traveling on the job, he had run out of places to go. These men, and they were almost all men, were the most at home at sea; sons and grandsons of fishermen and merchant marines. This was their chosen way of life and they were in it for the long haul. Despite their position and power, the officers, jocks in the truest sense, always had to prove they were the best, the idea of them losing in anything to other members of the crew, especially cruise staff, was inconceivable and intensely embarrassing. Their true colors always came out during the annual rigged crew volleyball tournament, officiated by Captain Gallo, insuring the officers a victory each year and a trophy in the Officers Dining Room. The monarchy had to preserve its crown at any cost.

Whereas, most crew members kept their distance from these officers and viewed them as superior, I got to know them personally and considered them to be like anyone else on the ship. One thing I had to admire about Americans is their love and devotion to deodorant, something the Italians did not hold dear to their hearts or armpits. Smelly Puff Ball was the name I had given to one Italian officer who stunk so bad, I could easily identify him by his noxious scent. Stepping into an empty elevator, I had only to take one whiff and knew Smelly had left his calling card. He was a little round hairy man with a bald head, and the gait of a weeble wobble, but he had the stink of thirty construction workers. Viva Italia.

Another staff division clad in similar pressed white uniforms were the pursers who ran the hotel side of the ship and were responsible for checking passengers into their rooms, selling shore excursion tickets, handling passenger complaints, and serving as the official bank during the cruise. Most pursers were in their 20s, college-educated and usually hailed from countries like England, Holland, Sweden and the United States. Unlike the Italian officers, they were pale, their bodies craved cannoli, not trophies, and they wore the hairstyle of the geeky nerdish order. The pursers worked long and hard and had the honor that no crew member wanted; lots of time spent going one-on-one with the passengers.

Week after week, tireless pursers answered the same questions and often not very clever ones. Our cruise director liked to end the week by reading his top ten list of stupid passenger questions. His personal favorites were: "Do the crew live on the ship?" "What do you do with the ice carvings after they melt?" and "Where does the ship get its electricity?" He liked to tell passengers to look for a giant electric cord at the back of the ship that ran all the way to Miami. Some of the less brain-endowed cruisers actually went to the back of the ship to look.

Eventually pursers burned out like most of their colleagues; dealing with passengers became a nightmarish task. It was at this time that I discovered a very interesting phenomenon called "distancing." Burnout was a normal phenomenon and merely part of a cycle witnessed in almost every staff member, especially pursers. At first they were excited and cheerful to meet the new crowds each week, but after a couple of months the passengers resembled irritating mosquitoes. The desire to squash them was hard to contain and for pursers the road to insanity had begun.

For this reason workers like myself developed defense mechanisms for dealing with them. "Distancing" meant defining passengers as "cones" who were a different and separate breed from the crew. I have been told by reliable sources that "cones" referred to *Saturday Night Live's* Coneheads, who were endlessly asked where they came from. Their standard answer was France. The only thing French about our passengers were the fries they ate. It was considered unpopular to actually congregate with the "cones" and if any of us actually got involved romantically with a passenger it was termed "coning." I never developed these attitudes completely, although I did experience the burnout. I enjoyed interacting with the passengers, mostly because they served as a link to the outside world, often they updated me on current events; the *USA Today*, the only major newspaper available in many Caribbean ports was strangling me with its paucity of information, superfluous polls, and pukish blue and green colors. The pursers seemed to have mastered the act of manipulation of a "cone" but despite their talents, these educated clean suited youths were often found during their precious time off in exotic ports scratching their heads and absentmindedly nodding at middle-aged couples from Topeka, Kansas.

One of my closest friends and confidants on the Ecstasy was a purser named Chris, an Icelandic man over six foot tall with golden blonde hair, dancing blue eyes and even chiseled features. Friends mean everything on a cruise ship. With them the ship can seem like summer camp, without them it can be a very lonely place. Despite the thousands of people that surrounded me each week, there was a severe paucity of individuals to connect with on a conversational level beyond ones favorite ice cream flavor or discussing what casino to visit on the next port of call. Chris was someone I could talk to on a deeper level and I felt close to him because in so many ways we were on the cruise ship for the same reasons and shared similar educations and upbringing. We were outsiders, both expecting to be on the ship for only a short period of time, always commenting on what we saw around us and aware that at any moment we had the capacity to pick up and leave. I spent countless hours with Chris talking about the politics of the purser department, relationships, the culture of Iceland and never once did we need to talk about the weather or favorite ice cream flavors.

He was the closest thing I knew to a "Romeo" on the ship. With his Robert Redford striking looks, he attracted the flirty eyes of many female passengers each day as he worked the front desk of the ship answering questions and offering directions. Without even trying, he had a suave demeanor and was not the least bit shy about inviting passengers to join him for a drink. "How do you do it?" I asked him one night. "I'll show you," he bounced back to me and so for a couple weeks another purser and I enrolled in his Romeo's School of Romance. I am happy to say I passed but not with the kind of grades I would have hoped. Some weeks he would be involved with older women, which he seemed to enjoy as much as the younger ladies he would entertain. Chris, despite his Scandinavian looks was not afraid to compete with the Italian fleet of romantic officers. He matched them in pick up lines, suave walking style down the promenade and in sheer guts and recklessness in approaching any desirable female within striking distance.

One week a large tour group from Iceland came onboard. Chris spent the week drinking and socializing with his fellow Icelanders that according to my calculations represented close to 1% of that country's population. Eventually Chris would be reassigned from the front desk to the crew deck where he became the crew purser, responsible for all the paper work of all the crew members on the ship. Often bottled up in a small room many levels below the passenger decks, he had less and less time to play the game of romance and eventually left the ship. We had talked of living off the ship together but as it would turn out my burnout factor came several months before his and only after I had left the ship did I learn that he too was planning his departure. Chris, like many of his fellow pursers, could not escape and was ultimately the victim of long hours of administrative work coupled with an intense barrage of passenger frustration.

Cruise staff, on the other hand, were blessed with little work and a lot of privileges. Not all cruise lines treat their staff the same, but Carnival was unusually lax with rules and regulations for crew and not very demanding in terms of work hours required. The only activities we could not do on the ship was gamble, dance, or sit at a bar and even if we sinned and violated one of these edicts there was little chance of real disciplinary action. Our cruise staff, mostly comprised of dancers, performed two shows a week and helped with certain activities throughout the week. The rest of my team were comprised of musicians, child counselors and a disc jockey. Life was quite good for the musicians who had the liberty to wake up late and linger during the day until they performed at night. Often you found them sunbathing, reading, or playing cards. The disc jockey had a similar setup but was required to work each night in the disco.

However, the best position was no doubt the production singers, the prima donnas of the ship. A male counterpart named Gene joined Charla, who I had met on the plane. Their only responsibility was to perform two shows a week and at most they worked 6 hours a week; the rest of the time was spent with their every need and desire granted quicker than an all powerful genie from a bottle. These singers were treated to the best rooms on the ship and were allowed as much vacation time as they wanted. Whereas, the salaries for most cruise staff range between $250 to $300 a week, a production singer brought in close to $800 a week.

Early in my journey, even before the plane had taken off from Washington D.C., I had met my first friend, Charla. We spent one night whispering in the hallway of a Miami hotel, swapping stories and sharing our fears about the adventure that lay ahead of us, so we had already formed a bond before joining the ship. Charla had just graduated from college and had spent the past summers as an entertainer in local amusement parks, a normal stepping stone for ship performers. A natural beauty, she had auditioned for a singer position without really imagining she would ever be hired even as a stagehand. Now she had landed her dream job and was savoring every satisfying moment. Her face was recognized throughout the ship for she was the star in this fantasy world and even though she liked to play down all the attention, it was obvious to all that she really loved it, basking in the glow of adulation.

Our relationship quickly became like brother and sister as we settled into the routine of cruise life. Whereas, romance was a seasonal event in my life, it preoccupied Charla's calendar. The first few weeks of the cruise for Charla played out like a soap opera as the two studs of the ship fought for the honor to have her as their girlfriend. On one side was Denzel, a Tarzan-type figure, a gorgeous aerobics instructor from Los Angeles who could have appeared as the leading man in any film, while his competitor was Johnny, the stylish, long-haired, hip hop disc jockey from Texas. Denzel had been discovered during one of his explosive aerobics classes in Los Angeles where he liked to climb the walls like a spider and holler primeval grunts. A cruise representative witnessed this insane spectacle and brought him aboard the cruise in a matter of weeks. Now he was electrifying, motivating, and shocking middle-aged women during their 45-minute aerobics classes on the M.S. Ecstasy, as well as, courting the beautiful and desirable Charla.

Each night Charla and I would go over the pros and cons of each man until finally the moment arrived to make a decision. Denzel's Spiderman abilities were to no avail as the charming, sweet-talking disc jockey won and eventually dated Charla for most of her time on the ship. When she wasn't performing, she spent her days lifting weights, reading fashionable ladies magazines like *Elle* and *Cosmopolitan*, sunbathing, watching old movies, gossiping and applying makeup. I never saw Charla without cosmetics. In fact, after a few margaritas she confessed she often wore it to bed like a good luck charm so that her boyfriends wouldn't see her without it. Her pillow must have been very colorful. Not too long after, I nicknamed her "Tammy Faye Charla" to her chagrin.

Her life was luxurious, of the rich and famous except on a smaller scale; yet there were moments I sensed a boredom in her eyes. There was only so much mascara one could apply. I would often hang out in her room drinking tea, watching the same old movies and generally admiring her overflowing supplies of makeup, jewelry and designer clothes. Over time Charla became my true confidant on the ship, the person whom I would tell all my secrets and fears. Each week we would head off the ship together to go to malls or to the beaches. Though we began our journey on the same day, Charla remained on the ship that fateful day I walked off. Our friendship continued beyond the ocean as I wrote her letters trying to find out the latest news on the ship. After two years on the high seas Charla also decided she had had enough of ship life and left the world of cruising to join the National Broadway Touring Company of *Miss Saigon*.

Johnny, Charla's successful suitor and the disc jockey on the ship, worked the hours of an owl, lounging, sleeping, sunbathing during the day and re-emerging at night to occupy the four-sided glass booth in the Stripes Disco. Johnny and I spent many hours in his fishbowl talking about our common problems and frustrations, always to the thumping of the loud rock tunes. Johnny was surrounded by the most interesting characters on the cruise, collecting each and every one of their business cards. He was obsessed with networking, planning for that time he would leave the ship and use every number and name he ever collected to start a new career in every state of the union.

Also extremely distrustful of the management of the cruise ship, Johnny was forever coming up with conspiracy theories of how "they" were trying to get him to leave. If the concept "burnout" applied to anyone on the ship, Johnny was the poster boy. Not equipped with the proper equipment or music, Johnny had been involved in a letter writing campaign with the main office in Miami for months trying to arrange to get more music. He was demanding a better selection of CDs and would settle for nothing less. Time and time again he had been turned down and eventually he began to buy music with his own money. The irony of a multi-million dollar cruise line unable or unwilling to buy a couple extra CDs seemed ridiculous and for Johnny it was a reason not to sleep at night. I tried to explain that Carnival's CEO, a kind very rich middle-aged Jewish gentleman in Miami had a lot to worry about. After all he headed a company with thousands of employees, directed the largest fleet in the world, and was responsible for a company worth billions. It was unlikely he was masterminding a plot to keep Madonna's most recent release from Johnny's turntable. "You're full of shit," was the most rational and printable response I could get from the long-haired paranoid schizophrenic DJ from Texas.

Soon matters became extremely tense as the main office requested him to stay on board during our one day at port in Miami to play music for groups touring the ship. This was the day off every crew member looked forward to each week and for months Johnny played cat and mouse with cruise authorities fighting this unreasonable decree. In time, Johnny would ultimately leave the ship several weeks before me and return to the topless clubs of Dallas where he started. In the years since I have worked on the cruise ship Johnny still keeps a spark of hope that one day he will return to work aboard a cruise ship with a proper supply of music and he probably will, a victim of a sick love-hate relationship.

For many of us working in the industry the attraction of cruise life became an addiction that was hard to leave. I met many people who have been on ships for five years or more and were simply terrified to get off. Gene, Charla's partner on stage, a black man in his thirties was closing in on 9 years of ship life. He had worked on every ship Carnival ever produced. The concept of grocery shopping, paying utility bills, cleaning an apartment were abstract ideas to a man that had spent nearly a decade on a floating hotel. He was a cruise co-dependent, functional at sea and a total wreck on land. He had tried to adjust to life in Philadelphia at one time and within a week was back at sea. Stories were told of how some of those who left had to rock themselves to sleep once they left the ship, withdrawal was painful and often unsuccessful. The responsibilities of living a normal life after being catered to on a ship was too much for many departees, and the cruise management, to their devilish delight, liked to use this fear of adjusting to land life as a weapon to keep us aboard.

The fly-ons enjoyed both living on the ship for a night or two and then returning to their land-based home. These performers would be flown to different ports where they board the ship for one or two nights and then leave at the next port. One fly-on act who became a good friend was Mickey, a break-dancer from Orlando, Florida who joined the cruise for three days each week as part of a three-person break-dancing team. Mickey, a stocky Hispanic looking man with olive green eyes and bushy brown hair, had been in the entertainment business since he was a kid. He talked with a kind of confidence that I rarely heard and preferred cruise shows to the jaded show business stunts he had become accustomed to like juggling at amusement parks or dressing up in big furry costumes for birthday parties. Like Chris, Mickey's sincerity and intelligence were limited commodities on a cruise ship, allowing us to talk about deeper issues removed from the day-to-day life of the cruise ship.

During my stint on the ship I always looked forward to his arrival to catch up on his adventures and talk about subjects I had been deprived of on the ship like philosophy, religion, careers, and current events. One night while sitting on the sofas in a public area of the ship Mickey began talking about all the assistant cruise directors he had met and his repeated conversations about getting off the ship and going into business for himself. Another co-dependent, cruise line junkie, I thought. "Promise me that one year from now you won't be having this same conversation with another assistant cruise director," I begged. He was silent, acknowledging the great cyclone of power cruise life held over anyone familiar with it. "Promise," I repeated. "I do, I swear," Mickey said with his usual intensity and breathed a sigh of relief.

The problem for Mickey was that the deal the cruise ship offered his group was almost too good to be true, earning enough money in just five minutes of performing so that they wouldn't have to work the rest of the week. The cruise ship was an exciting place for three days and it wasn't just the money that made it enticing. Each break-dancer had their share of romance waiting for them on the ship each week. Mickey was accompanied by Matt, a lanky six-footer famous for his jet black sky-pointing hair a la Don King that rose a good 30 inches from his scalp and by Tim, a blonde surfer boy with good looks and bad-boy behavior. They invented a game they would play each night in the disco whereby the dancing trio walked up to an attractive woman who quickly recognized them as the break-dancers and asked her to reveal which one of them she would most like to kiss. They kept a running score each week and the game would often end by the dancer kissing the passenger amidst cheers. Mickey would remain a friend after I left the ship, his break-dancing trio made it to the halftime shows of the NBA and to the stages of Las Vegas, but eventually he broke off on his own to pursue a career in music.

In numbers, the cruise staff and all the entertainers only made up a small part of that 800 member crew, the majority of employees on the ship were cleaners, cabin stewards, waiters, or deckhands. Working nonstop, these workers had very little time to get off the ship and enjoy the ports. In many cases they worked under intense stress. One evening while eating dinner I witnessed just how hot this pressure actually got. All waiters begin their time on the cruise ship as trainees in the crew dining hall until their managers feel they are ready to move upstairs to wait on the passengers. On this evening a group of Indian trainees were setting up a table, when a British manager strode into the dining room. He looked at the table with its plates and glasses carefully arranged, the silverware grouped neatly and then raised his head to glare at the waiters who stood anxiously in front of him. "What is this?" he shouted. Heads turned towards the booming voice. Then without a warning he grabbed the tablecloth and pulled it off the table, sending the plates and silverware flying all over the place. "This is a disgrace, how many times do I have to teach you guys!" I stood transfixed by the humiliating debacle and the tension was visibly tangible in the room as his tantrum lasted for a few minutes before he disappeared into the kitchen. Without a word, the waiters sheepishly picked up the silverware and broken china and reset the table. I could not believe what I had just seen, and with the different nationalities I couldn't help but think I was witnessing colonialism all over again. This demeaning tone in many of the managers on the ship was widespread.

This type of manager really pissed me off. Since I couldn't really do anything about them I developed my own personal strategy of retaliation, bumping into them purposely in the hallways and giving them the evil eye whenever I had the opportunity. When I saw them heading in my direction, their arrogance would erupt a well of anger inside of me. In my mind they deserved to be punished for the way they treated their employees.

My greatest run in with management occurred during a time on the ship when I lifted weights and drank protein shakes in a desperate attempt to increase my size and mass. I was the skinny guy about to become Charles Atlas if I could just get enough of these magical protein concoctions down my gullet. I arranged with one of the bartenders to get a couple of plastic containers used to mix drinks for my protein shakes.

Each evening I sneaked into a crew kitchen close to my room and stole a little milk to mix with my protein powder and made a shake. As I left the kitchen this particular night I bumped right into Sergio, the Manager for Food and Beverages on the ship. A stiff-postured Spanish man with undulating locks of black hair, Sergio at first gave me a friendly smile but when his eyes drifted to the stolen container of milk in my hands, his look changed to one of bewilderment soon followed by disgust. Standing two feet away from the man who was in charge of everything that had to do with food on the ship, I knew I had a problem. "I don't understand, where did you get that container, young man," he asked," his voice rising with each word. "From a bartender," I mumbled incoherently. "I don't understand," he repeated. It was close to one in the morning and I was feeling on edge. I quickly turned around and sprinted to a door leading into a long corridor that then separated into a maze of hallways. I knew I could lose him and if he wanted these containers so badly he was going to have to chase me down. He didn't even try and within minutes I was free to return to my room victorious, to celebrate with my hard-won protein shake.

Like the many decks below, the staff on the M.S. Ecstasy was separated by class, rank, title, nationality; for some aboard this was an invitation to arrogance and abuse, for others like Captain Gallo it was handled with charm and dignity. Regardless of the many differences between the hundreds of workers that kept the cruise vessel afloat each day, there was a great bond of citizenship that we all shared, we were sisters and brothers of the sea, and when our floating city harbored each Sunday morning in Miami, we looked at each other with the unspoken understanding that this was just a pit stop, a short break, home was somewhere else and soon the fog horn would call us back.

Chapter 5
Is There Love on the Love Boat?

"Would you happen to know where the buffet is?" she asked so innocently as I turned the corner, rushing back to my cabin after hosting a late night event. I had been turning the corner full speed so there was no way to avoid her. Our bodies were now inches away as we each checked for fender bender damages. She had a pleasing face, midwest, wholesome, a little bit pudgy, but her smile was radiant. Without backing off, she repeated, "Do you know where the buffet is?" I looked her right in the eyes and without hesitation answered, "I am the buffet," and so our night began. She didn't seem surprised by my response at all. She just grabbed my hand in hers and we began walking. I asked, "what are your plans for the evening?" with a dash of authority. After all I was wearing my standard Carnival uniform: a blue blazer, white pants, and white shoes, punctuated by my little Carnival name tag. I was about to commit a crime, a high crime of the sea. The first of three golden rules of the ship for all crew members was absolutely no romance with passengers. It was a rule that was spoken about, written about, talked about and most importantly violated by the select few. Up to now I had heard the stories, wondering how it really happened. I was beginning to find out.

When these mammoth cruise ships are built in the shipyards of Italy there must be a love fairy that sprinkles dust of romance into their hulls and spirits. The names of Carnival's fleet spoke for itself, the M.S.

51

Fantasy, the M.S. Sensation, the M.S. Ecstasy, the M.S. Celebration, the M.S. Fascination. It was a labor of love. I continued to lead my newly found date around the ship, walking faster and faster as we inhaled the clean sea air. Strains of Abba's Dancing Queen filtered in from the disco, but mostly it was the crashing of the waves against the side of the boat that served as background music to our conversation. "Where are we going?" Susan asked. Later I would find out the details. A nurse from Philadelphia, recently broken up, avid drinker, Susan had decided to vacation with a group of friends from college. As we passed a blue door emblazoned with the words, "KEEP OUT," I tried to impress her with my knowledge of the ship. "That's the entrance to the crew swimming pool, maybe we can go there sometime." What I didn't tell her was the pool only measured 8 feet long and closed at 6 p.m.. I left the details to her imagination. Favorite music, high school, brothers, ex-boyfriends, something about seasickness, her words were getting lost in the wind. We walked down a narrow deck, the white railing to our side, the wind whipping up against us, pulling my shirt tight against me. We stopped and faced each other. Snuggled within a wind tunnel, I dug my hands deep into her shoulders while alternating my stares out at the endless black sea and burying my head into her hair. I inhaled her smell, though there were traces of disco laced smoke. It smelled sweet as perfume and its softness brushed against my face.

She squeezed my hands and leaned in for a kiss. I smelled the slightly sour alcohol on her breath as I am sure she could on me. The kiss was comforting. Her hair blew wildly in all directions. We were totally alone and heard only the tapping of canvas covers against the hard body of the ship and the loud snapping of the waves. From the darkness I heard distant Italian voices, officers no doubt, probably committing the same sins I had been so actively involved in for the last hour. My nurse practitioner let out a sigh, and pushed me away. "Let's go back to your cabin." We grabbed each other's hands and sprinted to my cabin.

The next day I had a hard time concealing my smile. Carnival had made it explicitly clear from the beginning that "relations" with passengers was strictly forbidden and would not be tolerated. Even before I had been hired, the Carnival Entertainment Director had mentioned specifically that romances with passengers was not professional and could be grounds for dismissal. But after a couple of months on the ship, it was clear that life at sea was not the professional world that top land-based management aspired to. Romance was happening everywhere on this ship, in the hallways, jacuzzis, bathrooms, stairwells—every dark or light corner of the ship was a potential spot for love. If you thought about the logistics of the ship, it was easy to understand. Close to 3,000 people were confined to a 13-story boat. Most of the cabins were tiny, and often passengers shared very close quarters with friends and family. No one wanted grandma to be part of the kisses. Most of the public space consisted of discos, restaurants, casinos, swimming pools or lounge areas. But I wasn't complaining and neither were any other crew members.

The romances with passengers was really one of the fringe benefits of working on the ship. You have your free room and board, free food, free trips to interesting ports, and your choice of 2000 passengers. Crew after all, even had their own word for these flings with passengers, "coning." You won't find it in a dictionary so I'll give you a Webster sentence. Matt, the purser said to his colleague, "I think I will go coning tonight. I'm in the mood for love." "Coning" would be defined as engaging in a romance with a passenger. There were thousands to choose from and the menu changed weekly. I must confess I was addicted to coning and the scene in general. Each Sunday the photographers of the ship would greet all the passengers before they boarded the ship for the ceremonial palm tree shot. Smiling tourists bedecked with a lei would stop for thirty seconds in front of a fake cardboard palm tree to have their photos taken. The photographers, not the most adept at covering their boredom, would snap away for hours at a time, grinning and yawning in strange tandems of muscular twitches. By Sunday evening their hard work would be exhibited on the walls of the Empress deck.

On the way to dinner, passengers would pass through the Hall of Pictures and conveniently be able to purchase multiple copies for ridiculously high prices. Monopolies are a bitch at sea. Crew members would also walk through this same hallway, only to them it was the Hall of Love. Surveying the walls, my fellow cruise staff, waiters, cabin stewards, porters and photographers would visually hunt for prospects in the upcoming cruises, possibilities for their coning adventures. Certain cruises were for the dogs; letdowns because of the scarcity of good-looking females. Other cruises would draw more and more spectators to this hall as they marveled at the many beautiful women displayed on the wall. A jolt of excitement would strike through the crew decks as word got out that the ship was full of babes. There may be a group of 500 Brazilian women or an unusually large number of bachelorette parties. It didn't matter.

It wasn't only the male employees either. The female dancers with their voluptuous physiques and Dallas cowboy cheerleader looks were a strange bunch. British hotties that pronounced their vegetables in ways that made tourists from Indiana squint with confusion, these girls strained the neck of every male cruiser, except their male dancer counterparts who were as gay as a Christmas ornament. The dancers were under Gestapo style weight restrictions, each with a contract and a weight they had to remain under or face the consequences. One dancer may have been eating too many pastries at the midnight buffets because she mysteriously disappeared after one of the famous monthly weigh-ins. It was for this reason that the dancers spent a lot of their time in the gym or munching on cereal in their cabins.

Samantha, the buxom blonde flasher from London was a star attraction. Just under six feet, Samantha was a big woman with a big mouth and an insatiable appetite for romance. Of all the dancers she seemed to carry the most love per pound, mostly in her breasts and butt. With no need for makeup, Sam was a dynamo who entangled many travelers into her mischievous and rather nasty web of love. She was known for two things, pulling up her shirt to show off her boobs to total strangers, and leading the dancers in violating the golden rule forbidding fraternizing with passengers. Pointing to a good-looking passenger, or "cone" as she called them, Sam in her spunky British accent would proclaim, "I'll have him," or her in certain cases. Samantha also liked to do splits on tables and jump into any body of water she saw, including water fountains in front of buildings or in shopping malls. She was a satiated Sharon Stone on crack, living on meaningless flings, cheeseburgers, cheap thrills, and living in a state of nirvana. All of the cones around her seemed rather happy too.

As Assistant Cruise Director, I often orchestrated romance. My first and most powerful weapon was my ability to order champagne whenever I wanted. I had the magic debit card, which I could present at any bar and demand as many bottles as I desired. Champagne was supposed to be the prize for the many events I hosted, but often I defined events on my own terms and used this privilege loosely. Sunday was the big night for champagne. Besides the opening night for the Hall of

Photos, Sunday was the first night on the ship and the big kick off for the Stripes disco. Stripes hosted the opening night Rum Swizzle Party. By the time most people arrived at the disco they were pretty much tanked and the Rum Swizzles just added to the effect. The disco stood at the end of the Promenade deck that was the Vegas of the cruise ship. Several nightclubs, restaurants and discos lined the deck; neon lit up the corridors. Small lottery booths manned by smiling cruise staff decorated the Promenade along with a constant barrage of bells chiming and coins dropping from the casino's slot machines. Every hour a loud yet barely discernible announcement would blare over the intercom from the cruise director offering cheery advice on shopping as well as the scheduling of shows and ports of call.

When walking down the Promenade everyone stared at each other. It was the national sport. At the end of the walkway you saw crowds formed at the entrance of the Stripes Disco, a 70s style disco with checkered floors and a large silver ball twirling slowly from the ceiling. The volume in the room was enough to make a stadium rock. There was no real way to communicate with the person next to you except by mouthing something or touching them, a very popular pastime in this part of the ship. It was my job to increase the amount of touching. This party was the first of many singles parties aboard the ship. Before 10 p.m., the disco was fully packed wall-to-wall with people full of hope for the evening. First, groups of men and women stuck to their corners, but then the dance floor came alive and eventually passengers paired off. The room started buzzing and writhing with some pretty bad dancing. Think of Michael Jackson's *Thriller* and add some strobe lights and a lot of white people. It was time to grab the microphone.

Entering the disco, carrying my pathetic bag of cruise ship-shaped plastic trophies, I headed directly to the disco booth, centered on the dance floor, to have a quick word with Johnny. I moved in slow motion, battling the gyrating crowd as I bumped up against the many party goers jammed together. Women looked back at me with flirtatious eyes as I gently touched their backs and moved closer to my destination. The room reeked of body sweat and stale cigarettes. Johnny was easy to spot by his shoulder length chocolate brown hair, dark blue blazer and cowboy hat that looked strangely out of place on this ship or anywhere but his home state of Texas. A former disc jockey in the sleazy strip joints of Dallas,

Johnny was a true cruise ship veteran. "Micha, look over at that fox," he said pointing to a gorgeous blonde woman bending over a barstool. As disc jockey, he always had the best view in the house.

As much as he complained about life on the cruise ship, for those brief hours when he was in the booth with the music blaring, surrounded by hundreds of dancing passengers, he seemed to have a good time. But Johnny was also on medication. Long Island Iced Teas to be exact. I could see he was already on his second for the evening. This explained the smile. It was his form of numbing. He had been on the cruise ship for way too long; he just couldn't get off. He talked about it, but he was getting close to a decade of living, breathing, eating, and crapping cruise ship life. He was that guy you heard about who after leaving the ship had to rock himself to sleep because he had become addicted to life at sea. I knew a couple other crew members who were also nearing ten years on the ship. Johnny was getting ready to celebrate his eighth anniversary at sea. He had served his time on nearly every Carnival ship. He liked to vent when I was around. "I'll be getting off this damn ship soon. I'm getting sick of this routine." I ignored it; I had been hearing it for so long. They should have had 12 step meetings on the ships, CA for Cruise Anonymous. Johnny would have been the first to sign up.

For now Johnny's therapy was four Long Island Iced Teas a night and a dose of big-breasted women pressing their bodies against his glass booth. This therapy is very effective. He was with a different woman each week; they lined up outside his glass cage at the end of the night. If I knew anything about music I would have been a disc jockey, but luck was not on my side. The Texan handed me the microphone with a long wire attached. I walked to the middle of the floor and as I spoke I heard my voice echo across the room. The Saturday Night Fever zombies on each side of me parted. "Welcome folks, aboard the M.S. Ecstasy, I am Micha Berman, your Assistant Cruise Director." I sounded like one of those used car salesmen, but no one seemed to care. "Are you ready to party?" The response was instantaneous, and I am sure could be heard all the way down the Promenade deck. This was it. Work all year so you can have one crazy week on a cruise ship and do whatever you pleased. Their screams contained months of frustration, boredom and repression. Johnny raised the lights a bit and the crowd squinted for just a second before they adjusted. I began my usual routine about how there were so many single people on the cruise and how everyone was looking for love. I ended with a "let the games begin." I randomly selected three men from the audience and then three women.

I had studied under a cruel and sadistic cruise director so I knew the tricks of the trade. Rule #1: choose men that looked weird, nerdy, arrogant, or over weight but always choose men that are sober. Rule #2: look for women that are well endowed, beautiful, or overweight and definitely drunk. Any of these combinations would work and in almost all cases they did. Drunken people, drunken audience, drunken disc jockey. I was the only semi-conscious one in the house and the truth was, most nights, I was buzzing from screwdrivers. Each couple received ten balloons; the women would blow the balloons up and place them between their seated male partner's legs and then bounce up and down on the balloons. The first couple to pop all ten of the balloons were the winners and awarded the coveted plastic trophy. If it sounds sexual, it was. One man lay on the ground and his partner, a tub of a woman, enjoyed grinding each and every balloon. "Women blow harder," I screamed as the balloon kept popping and the screams of the audience got louder. The same jokes worked each and every cruise; it was an easy living.

I also felt the eyes of passengers watching my every move. This was my first night out, too. Shortly after the cruise got underway, I quickly became a recognizable face, a mini celebrity you may say. As I walked into the disco one night, I noticed a group of women dancing by themselves in a corner. Still early in the evening, the disco was half empty with Kool & the Gang's *Celebration* blasting from the sound system. One woman with raven black hair caught my eye. Her tight blue top showed signs of perspiration, wet circles under the armpits. She was dancing up a storm. Sweat on men is sick, dirty and smelly. On the right woman it is downright sexy. This woman fell under the "allowed to show sweat rule." She was gorgeous. She had short hair and looked tomboyish, a style that always attracted me. What the heck, I told myself as I walked toward the group and to this woman in particular. I had recently completed my pre-pickup routine which all took place in the privacy of my cabin. My whole life I have been nervous going to bars, walking up to completely strange women, and most of all standing amongst hundreds of single men all competing for the chance to approach that one beautiful woman on the dance floor. College was the worst as I had spent most of my weekends standing in fraternity houses surrounded by thousands of inebriated brothers, but now wearing a uniform, I had finally gained my confidence and most importantly had discovered a secret weapon.

Sitting in my cabin I found that liquor could be my savior. Mixing a couple screwdrivers while I listened to Kenny G tunes relaxed me for an evening of flirting. The hastily made drinks gave me a nice buzz, eliminating any hesitation or excess rumination, which had always got in the way of a good time. The Kenny G tunes can only be seen as feeding my dysfunctional taste for America's most hated music. Think of middle-aged white male musicians. Now think of white middle-aged male musicians that are the butt of all jokes. Voila! Those are my favorites, Neil Diamond, Barry Manilow, John Denver and the king of the pack, Kenny G. For as long as I can remember, I have loved Barry Manilow and have been humming *Rocky Mountain High*. As a seven-year-old I would lay on the carpet for hours listening to Bobby Vinton. It was a sign of things to come. I tried to hide it for a while out of embarrassment, but I finally came out of the closet and embraced this music without regard, even proclaiming to the world my love for musicals. *Annie, Gypsy, Showboat* and *Chorus Line* rounded out my favorite tunes. This may have explained why my closest confidants argued that I really didn't like tomboys, but I lusted simply for boys. Not true I told them. Just shut up and let me listen to *I Write the Songs*.

I stared at the woman on the dance floor. The disco was beginning to fill up as Madonna's *Like a Virgin* whipped the crowd into a frenzy. Matt, a purser friend, saw my approach and followed in line as support or maybe as competition. This could get nasty with Matt dressed in his newly clean white purser uniform, freshly pressed and practically shining on the dance floor. It was hard for me to compete. This was like some kind of wildlife public television program where the animal with the brightest colors wins the female. In this case I just hoped to make it over to her first and pop the question, "Would you like to share some Korbel with us?" She and her friends took the bait. As we sat down at one of the cocktail tables that surrounded the dance floor, I jockeyed for position. I needed to be the alpha male and won a seat next to Julia, a college student from New York City. Immediately we had great chemistry as we chatted on about movies, religion, death, and family. There was an incredible synergy between us, we kept eye contact and kept inching closer to each other with every word. It was such deep conversation and yet so utterly useless.

I was always the guy who had the most spiritual and connected conversations and at the end of the night went home alone. It's the nice guy syndrome. Kenny G appeared over Julia's shoulder with his long goofy hair and pelican nose. "Get with the program, Micha; she digs you." I stopped in mid sentence. Let's take a walk on deck. She agreed and once again I was arm and arm with a beautiful woman. Within seconds the pulsating breath of the disco was behind us. There was a slight chill on deck as Julia leaned her body against mine as we walked, our small steps in synch. I was gaining ground on Johnny. Soon conversation had turned stupid and silly. It was incredible, we were laughing and I knew I was on the right track. Thanks, Kenny.

Julia wanted to go back to the disco and dance. Dancing was strictly off limits to crew members. This was the second golden rule. Big Brother was always watching. Big Brother, that bunch of Indian security guards recruited by Carnival and paid very little to patrol the cruise ship. Security had the distinction of wearing the ugliest uniforms on ship. Off green with a tinge of yellow, the full uniform appeared to be a mix between navy garb and a South American dictator. Each had a walkie-talkie on their side and a small billy club. Their confidence level was equal to a three-legged turkey on the eve of Thanksgiving. While I never saw them perform any feats of bravery, I did learn some good chicken tikka recipes from them, and during my moments of boredom, which was what they experienced most of the time, they were great to pass the time with.

Actually security was pretty good at finding crew members that were up to no good. They weren't very successful at stopping the indiscriminate sex, but they did stop crew from dancing and drinking while sitting at a bar. Tonight I felt reckless so I headed back to the dance floor holding Julia's hand tightly. The night was magic even with my lack of discretion. Some crew members' lack of discretion would haunt them forever. For instance there was the Caribbean cabin steward who was caught by Big Brother leaving a passenger's cabin and fired on the spot. But he was a recidivist with a long history of leaving passengers cabins. In fact he was always proud to show me the many pictures of all the women he had slept with, from Florida, Illinois, Georgia, and Nevada. The list was endless. This was his second family; his first consisted of a wife and five children all living in Nicaragua. It was safe to say the families never met. I was not a repeat offender, was not as flagrant and I did not have a wife or child.

Also ship security had a double standard. They were much tougher on the lower ranked members of the crew. Italian officers could do whatever they wanted. Cruise staff, musicians, dancers were pretty much immune, like diplomats; however, waiters, busboys, cabin stewards were punished with swift justice. Fortunately I had diplomatic immunity; I needed it this night. If I was caught, I would have to plead not guilty by reason of temporary insanity induced by Kenny G.

We did end up in Julia's cabin on the Mezzanine deck, dangerous territory for any crew member. After some innocent fun I collapsed on the bed and fell asleep in a matter of seconds. Later that night I recalled a strange dream. I was looking out a window and having an incredibly volcanic urge to pee. It was painful. I began to look for the bathroom. The surroundings were unfamiliar, everything was out of place. I knew it was a dream but the need to urinate was as real as it could be; it was a nightmare as I felt the walls and turned corner after corner unable to find the toilet. I walked faster, hyperventilating, and generally panicking. Frantically searching, I spotted a glass on a counter next to a candle. I grabbed the glass, pulled my underwear down and began to pee. The glass filled quickly and I could feel the warmth of the urine in my hands, and looked down in time to see it overflowing. I snatched another smaller glass and kept peeing. It felt so so good. It was the kind of release where you need several minutes after it is done to just stand there and savor how good life really is. I breathed deeply and just smiled. I carried the glass somewhere and then things became fuzzy.

It was only a dream, but when I woke up in the morning next to Julia, I had an odd sensation. Deep in my stomach I knew something was wrong, it felt too real. I jumped up from the bed and took a quick glance around the small cabin. This was too weird, it couldn't have happened. But then I saw the candle on the ledge. "I need to check your bathroom real quick," I told Julia, trying not to act suspicious. She seemed half-asleep. I ran to the bathroom and peeked in. There stood a glass on the sink, it was a wineglass with yellow liquid sitting innocently at its base. This was no ordinary Napa Valley Chardonnay, this was my own private vintage. To make matters even stranger, next to the glass was a small contact lens container. Could I have peed in both? "What's going on in there?" Julia asked. I ignored her, buying time, this was sick. Could I have sleep peed? I had stumbled upon a new habit of mine, and maybe a new scientific discovery, sleep-peeing. Maybe I should have applied for the Guinness Book of weird and wacky records. I realized this wineglass was Julia's to take home, so I rinsed it well, getting rid of any yellowish residue. I could see her trying a new wine in a couple months at one of her fancy New York parties. "This one tastes a little bit acidic, but I like it." Hey Julia, now that's a real "penile-noir." For Julia, a part of me would always be with her; she seemed fine at breakfast. Good-byes were in order.

When it comes to peeing, crapping, and other bodily functions, I was listed in many tourist guides, almanacs, and yearbooks as strangely obsessed to certain rituals. Since elementary school I had always been terrified to sit on toilets that I couldn't call my own. It was my pot or no pot. This, of course, created havoc for my parents as well as school officials. Often my parents received phone calls about their son turning blue in the face because he refused to use the school bathroom. Only later in life did I uncover the wonderful and genius invention of a U-shaped piece of paper that conveniently fit atop the toilet seat. Maybe I wasn't the only one out there who didn't want my butt sitting on wet dirty creepy toilet seats. Often in many of the ports in the Caribbean we docked, I avoided the public bathrooms all together. I simply used nature as my bathroom; there were plenty of jungles. In the woods out of view, I relaxed and did my business. With the wonderful technologies of the modern age, I forgot how wonderful it was to squat down in the woods and deliver the goods. In the Caribbean I got in touch with my waste products. This may sound like an infomercial, "Getting In Touch With Your Fecal Matter by Micha Berman." I thought of all the strange and beautiful places I had gone to the bathroom, the woods in Ocho Rios, the mountains of St. John, the waters of the Cayman Islands. I could have written a coffee table book of "One Hundred of the Most Beautiful Places I've Crapped." With my new sleep-peeing habit, I could have followed this book with, "One Hundred of the most Beautiful Places I've Sleep-Peed Including Your Mother's Denture Cup."

After Julia it was back to the hard work of assistant cruise director. Women smashing their butts against balloons was only a small part of my job. I also had to devote considerable energy to the dirty dancing competitions on board. Three couples each night were chosen, individually matched only moments before their performance. They had thirty seconds to get as raunchy as they could and they did. Once again my skills as Cupid came in handy. My magical fingers pointed to the lucky or unlucky female or male participant. Men and women went through every possible sexual position imaginable.

Romance is hard work and required lots of food for energy. I couldn't help but think that was one of the reasons cruise ships served buffets 24/7. Seafood buffets, pasta buffets, Mexican buffets, pastry buffets, the list was endless. If pigging out at the grand buffet of the evening wasn't enough, there was even a late night buffet for those late night/early morning stomachs with legs scouring the cruise ship. Speaking of stomachs, mine was starting to bloat. I felt a slight queasiness as I shut my eyes, this time in the safety of my own bed. I had a super sensitive stomach. Medical schools will fight over my body when I die, all rushing to dissect my organs and figure out why this guy displayed symptoms not seen in any other human species. Call me a hypochondriac, but I went into a panic if my pants felt just a little too tight.

To make things worse I ate a lot of junk. I held the college record for ordering-out the most consecutive nights, 45 orders of gyros, onion rings and Caesar salad. Their total grease count enough to fill a milk jug. I always remembered Sunday nights with the family watching *Sixty Minutes* and eating Roy Rogers Roast Beef sandwiches. This is where my love affair for eating out began. I loved any food not cooked in my kitchen, even airplane food, and had an even more dangerous liking for fatty, fried and generally heart-attack-inducing treats. This stomach took a turn into the Twilight Zone as I sometimes experienced sharp anal pains, which struck me in the most inopportune times. For years I suddenly got a piercing sharp pain in my butt, like someone stuck a spear up there and jabbed me. I could be standing in a line and without warning, the spear came like a jolt of electricity. I looked like an epileptic crack-induced scarecrow from the Wizard of Oz. My limbs bent in strange ways, I grimaced and my whole body straightened up. Not always the greatest turn on for my dates. The doctors checked it out; I was fine but no real explanation. I tried my best to cover it up, but some ladies got to see the show.

New Year's Eve on the cruise ship brought me together with an exotic beauty, a Brazilian woman named Alicia. At 10 o'clock I felt the first sign of stomach pain. Not again I thought, what a way to start the New Year. I tried to ignore it, but a couple minutes later even more discomfort. I removed my belt without Alicia even noticing. At 11 p.m. the first beads of sweat appeared on my forehead and it was clear Super-sensitive-stomach sickness was upon me. The symptoms could not have been disputed. Alicia was touching me more and more. 11:15 p.m. I ran to the bathroom, hunching over trying to cover up my pain. Alicia must have thought I was inventing some new funky dance or maybe she dismissed my behavior as a cultural thing. I gained my composure again and assured my beautiful companion that everything was fine. " It must be so exciting to work here," she whispered to me prying for more details about what ship life was really like. I had spent four weeks studying Spanish, imagining a moment like this with a lovely Latin lover, only to realize my unfortunate luck that Brazil is the only country in Latin America that speaks Portuguese. Alicia's English wasn't bad, she skipped words every once in a while, but I was more than forgiving. Her face was perfectly proportioned, her eyes large and tortoise colored, her nose cute as a button. Her lips were amazing, doused with lipstick and they were huge. I explained how lonely it was at sea when suddenly the sharp anal pains arrived.

I rushed to the bathroom before Alicia saw my body jerking. I closed the bathroom door behind me and looked into the mirror. Not tonight, just leave me alone. Anyone watching me may have thought I had multiple personalities; no, I was just experiencing anal thrusts from an imaginary weapon. Very normal stuff. I ran back out to the dance floor. "Are you alright, sweetheart?" she asked me with her sweet Portuguese accent. It was 11:30 p.m.. My body tensed up. She looked at me baffled. I turned and retreated again to the bathroom. I was becoming a regular visitor. This time when I locked the door I removed my pants as well as my shirt. Now I was in my underwear. I breathed deeply as I lay naked on the floor, the cool tiles tingled my back. It was 11:45 p.m., fifteen minutes from the New Year. I heard the crowd getting rowdier and wanted to make it back to Alicia and get that special Brazilian kiss at the stroke of midnight. I deserved it. Although it was looking bleak, I would even take Brazilian CPR. I didn't look like the coolest guy at the party as New Years Eve approached, staring at the white putty ceiling, feeling the coldness of the floor on my exposed butt. Still Alicia had no clue her date was indisposed. 11:55 p.m., it was time for action. I pulled my pants back on and ran out to the dance floor. Three - two - one. Happy New Year. Alicia grabbed me close and delivered the promised wet kiss.

Clearly women like Alicia came aboard looking for romance, and for many the ultimate fantasy was a cruise ship fling with those of us who worked on the liners. There was something magical, mystical, romantic and steamy about meeting a certified seaman. I never believed it before, but I do now; men in uniform attract women. The M.S. Ecstasy was ample proof. Still for all the romance on the ship, it was often short and unfulfilling for crew members in the larger scheme of things, especially for the ones that had been on ships for years, one-night, two-night, three-night stands didn't really provide real companionship. That's where the crew bar came into play. A small room out of sight from most passengers, the crew bar was most importantly a bar, but also had other forms of entertainment like pool tables, ping-pong tables, dartboards, and music. The walls were plastered with a strange mixture of old posters from the different cities of Italy, courtesy of the Italian officers, and advertisements for beer. An oasis where passengers were not allowed, the crew bar was a place for crew members to get drunk together and seek companionship. Everyone in this room had a drink in one hand and their other hand on a colleague catching up on the gossip of the day. Crew members dated crew members, but life at sea had its dangers as anyone could be transferred at a moment's notice; couples were not spared. There was a second problem, a big one. Over 90% of the crew were male and for the male dancers this was heaven, but for everyone else that meant slim pickings. Once in a while a romance blossomed, but it was few and far between. I knew of a casino dealer who married a dancer. Their wedding took place on a Caribbean island and lasted 2 hours, just enough time to do the vows and make it back to the ship. These relationships rarely lasted.

But for many of the men, the passengers were not a real possibility due to the strictly enforced "no relations" rule for lower ranked crew members and there were not enough women crew members to meet. What could they do? I found out at one port when I discovered my favorite jerk chicken center was actually a jerk chicken prostitution center. Every two weeks our ship docked in Ocho Rios, Jamaica. Not too far off from where the passengers disembarked, in a busy intersection of trees, sat a wonderful wooden shack selling the finest jerk chicken I had ever tasted. Each dish of chicken was served with a greasy bowl of heavily salted french fries on a cardboard tray. This gem was not known to passengers. Crew members flocked to this joint to eat; at least that's what I thought. It wasn't until I had eaten there for a couple of months that I noticed the crowds were all men, and often lower ranked crew members. They popped out of the bushes magically and often disappeared into the thick forest surrounding the chicken shack. When I looked a little closer I saw it wasn't just jerk chicken being served, it was a service center for sex. It was hard to enjoy my chicken dinners after that; seeing all the bushes rattle around me took my appetite away.

Passengers rarely had to pay for sex, after all they were surrounded by romance. For the most desperate, loneliest and least socially equipped, there was a singles service called "Connections" which brought aboard 30 or so singles from every cruise and ran events to help match up individuals. I always found this group a bit peculiar. I mean the whole cruise ship was a singles party, still these folks needed help and were willing to pay for it. Tom, a single man in his forties, was their host. Tom's face looked like Mars, acne scars of his teenage youth marked every inch of his face. It was like looking at the bark of a tree and telling its age. With Tom's face you read the history of his teenage pimples and all the embarrassment it contained. I had my share of pimples too and maybe like Tom had played "pop the pimple" just a bit too often. I used to surgically operate on the little white things right in front of the mirror and watch them hit the glass and splatter. Thanks to a good dermatologist my face was in recovery, but maybe Tom and I had something to talk about after all. His face told other stories. He looked like the kind of man who was happy all the time, a smile planted on his face. I couldn't stand him. I always thought that people who are always happy, perky, high on life, well there's something wrong with them. Either they were high on drugs, totally brainwashed by some cult, or serial murderers. "Hey Micha, how you doing," he chirped as he passed me in the hall.

I got to know Tom over the many cruises we took together, he was clean and sober, not a member of a cult, so I concluded he was a serial killer. Once when I dropped off a letter for him at his cabin, a young woman answered the door. She was in a bathrobe and had a smile to match his. I recognized her face as a member of "Connections." So I had found Tom's secret. He was hoarding all of "Connections" single ladies for himself. No wonder he was as jolly as Santa Claus. He was leading the lonely, defenseless lambs to his lair of love. It was all so clear to me now. "Say hi to Tom for me," I told the happy lamb in the door. Like I said, everybody was doing it.

It was true that Princess Cruises has the claim to the title of the "Love Boat." If you think back to the characters of the *Love Boat* series, they all seemed rather obsessed with romance. There was Isaac, the bartender with his droopy eyes and all of those hackneyed pick-up lines. There was Gopher, who strained his neck every time a woman with two legs walked by. The Doctor who prescribed just a bit too much medicine to the lovely ladies visiting his office and finally even bald Captain Stubing who in his private moments cried into his handkerchief pining for the perfect woman to step into his life. These were romance-starved men willing to do anything to get a lady to share a night of romance under stars, including using the persuasion of their uniform as well as a nice cold glass of champagne. Sound familiar? The M.S. Ecstasy was no love boat, but it was pretty close. From cabin stewards, to band members, to dancers, everyone was doing it. Far off in the Italian shipyards a new Carnival ship was being built, the fairy of love was getting ready to sprinkle her dust, and closer to home the M.S. Ecstasy was getting ready to sail again.

Crazy Cruise Trivia
Did you know?

In 1853 Cornelius Vanderbilt decided he needed a bigger ship

to take his family on vacations.

Hence with 500,000 dollars he launched the

2,500 ton North Star Ocean Liner

with his own private crew

including a

clergyman,

doctor and

purser.

Chapter 6
Ports, Ports, and More Ports

It's quite a scene. Passengers everywhere studying their tour books, maps, and travel brochures. As the ship nears its first port of call each passenger is consumed by their imagination, their buffet-filled brains processing how they will spend their ideal day in the Caribbean. Some will go shopping, others to the beach and a few will visit historical sites, but one thing is certain, they will not have a lot of time; the average time in port is not more than six to seven hours. Once the ship docks the footrace to see who can get off the ship first begins. Younger more versatile honeymoon couples with their spanking new tennis shoes and sex-driven adrenaline are the first to cross the threshold, followed by the more casual travelers and finally the walking infirmed, the seniors getting their last look at their cabin bathrooms before they head out on their adventure. It's a fancy Noah's Ark reversed, but much louder, chaotic and a bit less smelly depending on the cruise. Excitement fills the air as the cruisers get their first breath of paradise and witness the radiant blue waters and postcard-perfect mountain vistas.

Our cruise ship switched between two routes, the Eastern Route and the Western Route. The Eastern Caribbean cruise consisted of the Bahamas, Puerto Rico, and the Virgin Islands, followed the next week by the Western Caribbean ports of Cozumel, Mexico, the Cayman Islands and Jamaica. The Western Route offered an endless list of delectable sins, partying in Cozumel, snorkeling in the Cayman Islands and dozing off on the white sandy beaches of Jamaica and indulging in the delicious food. The Eastern Route was more refined, gambling in the posh casinos of San Juan, Puerto Rico, shopping for bargains in the bazaars of Nassau, Bahamas and finally a round of golf and fine dining in the Virgin Islands. Working two itineraries was a blessing, after all I could see six different ports in two weeks. For others in the business they had the unfortunate fate of seeing the same island every two days.

For the first couple of weeks I too was quick to rush off the ship to discover these new and exciting islands. Curious to see everything, I studied *Fodor's*, *Frommers*, *Lonely Planet* and every other travel book out there, occupying my days in port walking the islands, exploring the beaches and restaurants and enjoying the historical sites. After several weeks my discovery phase ended; the ports had become familiar places. Coming to the ports each week was like coming home. I knew all the places to go and was getting to know many of the people. The islands lost much of their fantasy appeal and took on a much more practical use. They became places to run my errands.

My best friend in port was no one other than the local telephone booth. Everybody working on the ship learns to accept a certain amount of isolation. Writing letters is one way to communicate with loved ones, but nothing beats hearing a familiar voice of a family member. The phone service available on the ship is too expensive for anyone to use, making ports crucial. In fact, many of the Caribbean ports have constructed telephone centers right off the dock to attract the international crew. As passengers come on and off the ship all day they are sure to see a flock of 30 to 40 phone booths, all occupied by a crew member transfixed in conversation. The wait could be as long as 30 minutes as conversations in Spanish, French, Hindi, and Italian all bled into a symphony of noise. On many occasions, I would rush off the ship minutes before it was leaving hoping to get in contact with somebody on the phone, knowing it might be a week before I got another opportunity. Most of my calls were made out of Puerto Rico, one of the few Caribbean Islands with affordable rates. The mother ship had some phones, but the price for calling was fit for rich folk and unless a crew member was in a life or death situation, it was not an option.

My biggest telephone surprise came one week when I received my monthly bill, usually under one hundred dollars. The amount under payment due was an unmistakable three thousand dollars. Splattered across the bill were several hundred phone calls to New Delhi, Bombay and other various cities in India, each lasting 20 to 30 minutes. Immediately, I knew what happened; the ship had many employees from India and obviously I had become a long distance phone sponsor for one of them. Someone had apparently been watching me closely in order to steal my phone card number and had engaged in the AT&T reach out and touch someone campaign. For brief moments after I discovered this scandal I imagined becoming Sherlock Holmes and checking the entire directory of Indian employees on the ship looking for the culprit; however, I never really pursued it. Of course, I did not have to pay the bill and from that point on I was more cautious when making my calls.

Ports meant something else very important to me—food! Growing sick and tired of the food in the crew dining room, I made it a personal rule to eat out at every port. In Mexico it was a little Italian bistro called Pizza Rolondos, in the Cayman Islands a German restaurant that served the juiciest Wienershnitzel and in the Virgin Islands, Madras, an Indian restaurant soon became my addiction. Most Americans take McDonald's for granted; however, after some time on the ship I was ready to bow at the altar of the Golden Arches and even began a food smuggling operation specializing in fast food. It was my personal Red Cross mission: transporting whoppers, burritos, french fries and other goodies into the safe haven of my cabin where an undernourished assistant cruise director could feed in private.

The first time I brought a bag of Kentucky Fried Chicken aboard I was not aware I was breaking a rule 'til the squad of security guards descended on me. Henry, an old retired cop explained in his exaggerated southern hickish drawl, "I'm sorry it's against ship policy to bring food on board, son." I had to challenge this absurdity. Refusing to eat another serving of mysterious beef stew or half-dead veal with stale potatoes, I took the offensive. "I would like to call the Staff Captain." The Staff Captain explained that as long as there were no beverages I could bring aboard prepared solid food; however, the policy changed weekly as every security guard had their own unique policy. After a while I hid the food in my shirt and avoided the hassle entirely. While other crew members struggled with their "ship rations," I enjoyed

Big Macs and Whoppers. Some of my colleagues avoided the crew dining room completely, creating kitchens in their cabins, a major violation of ship policy. Electrical appliances like refrigerators, microwaves, hot pots were all forbidden in our cabins; however, Charla like others, developed ways of hiding their secret supply of kitchen supplies from security. Each couple of weeks I participated in a room inspection of cruise staff, along with a security guard knocking on each door asking for permission to enter. We waited for minutes at a time at each door as the sneaky criminals covered their kitchen appliances with blankets or sheets, and shoved everything else under the sanctuary of their beds. It was routine, we all knew what was going on and few arrests or executions were ever made.

Despite the fact that I spent a great portion of my time on the islands dining, shopping and making calls, it was impossible to ignore the magic qualities of the Caribbean. The moment I stepped off the ship, I became a civilian again, returning to the world I once knew, a place with no curfews, no geographic boundaries, no limits on food, dancing, relationships and no uniform requirements. It was a life that you learn not to take for granted once you have lived on a cruise ship for a couple of months, and those precious six to seven hours rose to spiritual levels as my months on the ship closed in on a year.

Ports like the Cayman Islands were spectacular, presenting me with opportunities of a lifetime. One of the most popular tours the cruise ship offered in the Caymans was the Sting Ray Tour. I decided to go along with a group of dancers to see what all the fuss was about. After a one-hour ride in burning temperatures on a small boat we arrived at our destination. The ocean stood still as a mannequin, transparent, a beautiful mix of blues and greens; it invited us into its realms. However, what made this area even more awesome was a large patch of black water which consisted of several hundred sting rays swimming in circular motions, each surveying their fellow creatures in straw hats leaning dangerously close to the side of the boat staring so rudely.

Everyone was handed snorkel gear and off we went into the ocean to join our stingray friends. I was terrified at first and for good reason. "This here is shallow reef which at night fills up and is a feeding ground for the sharks," the local tour guide said, with a smirk on his face, and his turtle green eyes squinted ever so little. The locals of the Cayman Island are a strange bunch, but their eyes are downright spooky, all look exactly the same. "No worries, you are safe during the day from the sharks," the guide emphasized. Like much of my generation that has been scarred by *Jaws* my imagination began to create visions of a shark biting off my legs and dragging me below the surface, chomping me to shreds and serving my appendages as stingray appetizers. Wiping these images from my mind I jumped into the sea of blackness, dipping my head into the water and marveling at this new world I was peaking into. The stingrays showed no fear as they came right up to me, inches from my face, as if to be petted. "This was absolutely incredible," I thought as I swam amidst these wild creatures of the sea.

The subject of sharks came up a lot on the cruise ship. I heard rumors that some of the engineers on the boat hung out at the rear of the ship throwing raw meat into the ocean to attract sharks. The story sounded intriguing but I never witnessed it. Johnny, the disc jockey, claimed to have seen a large black shadow in the ocean that could only have been a shark, but he also claimed Watergate was nothing compared to what was happening in Carnival's Miami offices and that Elvis was once a passenger on the Ecstasy. So fascinated by his many sightings of sharks and music legends, he got into the habit of carrying a video recorder around with him on deck, ready to film the next Caribbean Loch Ness Monster.

When not swimming with stingrays, I played golf in the Virgin Islands. Each time our ship docked in St. Thomas I arranged to be off the ship as early as possible in order to take a cab to a golf course called Mahogany Run, considered to be in the top 100 most beautiful golf courses in the world. It became my second home as I enjoyed the cruise employee discount, $15.00 for a round on this stunning course with tee shots on cliffs and spectacular 360 degree views of the ocean, which cost others their next of kin. I felt like I was on *Fantasy Island* driving around in a golf cart with a big fat cigar in my mouth with no one in sight. My golf game never rose to the miraculous nature around me but it was unbridled pleasure. "What did I do to deserve this," I pondered amusingly."

Less exotic than the Cayman Islands or St. Thomas, Puerto Rico was like visiting any American city. It had all the luxuries I longed for including large shopping malls, legitimate book stores, coffee shops and large impersonal hair salons. Many items easily accessible on land became much tougher to find while living at sea. In particular I missed the opportunity to see movies on the big screen. Fortunately, one shopping mall in San Juan, Puerto Rico had a large movie complex with the most recent American films, each about two to three months behind in terms of release, but beggars can't be choosers and I was quick to line up for my ticket and popcorn.

Like Puerto Rico, Cozumel, Mexico provided a wonderful opportunity for nightlife. In Cozumel passengers and crew members joined together for a night of unlimited drinking at a loud, rambunctious "dive" called Carlos and Charlies. Walking into the club, you saw drunk men and women, mostly cruise visitors from our ship; as well as, the Royal Caribbean Fleet that arrived the same day, dirty dancing on table tops, forcing large quantities of every conceivable liquor down each other's throats. Add in some loud Rock & Roll music and some drunk people going to the bathroom in the street and you pretty much have the feeling for Carlos and Charlies on a typical night, an annoying sight but the lifeblood of the local economy. Of course, the difference between a drunk patron and a drunk passenger is that the passenger has to be on a cruise ship by a certain time. In Cozumel it was 1 a.m. and due to shallow water around the dock, the only way to reach the cruise ship was to take smaller boats called tenders. The last tender left at 12:45 a.m. and on average two passengers were left in town each week. "Don't forget to bring your cameras," Gary would remind all passengers spending the night at Carlos and Charlies. A passenger would always ask why. "Because there is no better picture than the M.S. Ecstasy sailing off into the distance," he would answer. A second later he would remark sarcastically, "Unless, of course, you're supposed to be on it."

Ports were like steaks. You had to decide how you wanted it done. For many passengers, the only part of the port or island experienced was the façade, the line of stores, restaurants, tourist information booths and bike rental stalls blanketing the main street. It was a Potemkin village, with no peasants, but smiling Caribbean merchants and American tourists reaching into their pockets for more cash. There were other choices for your steak besides rare. Behind this façade each island had a vibrant culture urging to be explored. Simply walking one or two streets beyond the glitter of the jewelry stores and banks revealed a world of natural wonder.

Cozumel, Mexico had its run down restaurants in broken-down concrete huts serving savory authentic chicken soup with flotillas of fresh vegetables and spices in every spoonful. San Juan, with its cozy and intimate cobbled streets showcased building after building of unique architecture and beautiful flower arrangements. Ocho Rios, Jamaica, for all its annoying and conniving salespeople, was a town rich in music and steeped in personality. Beyond the hustle and bustle of the town was a land of jungles, rainforests, and incredible wild life.

In the end, however, my favorite port was Miami, for it always felt like home. I savored my hours in Miami. This was my day to catch up on unfinished business. It also happened that Sandy, a good friend of mine was working in Miami for a year and routinely picked me up at the port to play golf, go swimming, or just hang out in his apartment to catch up on gossip. As I left the ship each Sunday, I would anxiously await his stories about two of our favorite subjects, women and movies. Both of us were major movie freaks often coordinating what films we saw during the week so that we could compare notes, sort of like Siskel and Ebert. It felt great to get in a car and drive away; it was a type of escape. One of the first times I met Sandy at the port I brought him on to the ship to see my new home.

Soon I discovered several ways to bring Sandy on the ship without anyone ever knowing he had come on, which in essence meant he could cruise for free. I thought of sneaking Sandy aboard but the risk seemed too great and his busy schedule never allowed for it anyway. I found out I wasn't the only crew member thinking about sneaking friends aboard the ship. Margie, a friend of mine who worked as a child counselor aboard the ship, had a sister who lived in Miami. One night after the ship had been several hours out of Miami I went to visit Margie to borrow some tissues. To my surprise her sister answered the door. "What are you doing here," I asked knowing full well I was looking into the eyes of a stowaway. "Micha, I snuck aboard and am planning to stay for a couple of weeks to save some money so I can fly home," she quickly explained. Before I could respond she clasped her hands together and looked desperately into my eyes. "Please let me stay, I promise you won't get in any trouble," she begged." Are you kidding me," I thought, I could lose my job. "Look, I am just going to pretend I did not see anything here tonight," I said as I turned my back and left.

I watched the both of them pull this stunt off for a couple of cruises. Walking to dinner with Margie and her sister, we ran into Gary. He looked at the sister with a confused face and said "I'm sorry we haven't met." Of course he knew all the cruise staff members but there were always visitors and there is just too much confusion aboard the ship to really keep track of who is who. A week later Margie's sister left the ship.

On the legal end, I was entitled to bring on immediate family for only two hundred dollars a week. Through some trickery my friends became brothers and soon the whole ship was astonished by the size of my family. Often I heard the comment, "Gee, he really looks like you." But I wasn't the only one breaking this rule. One unfortunate cruise staffer was caught kissing their "sister". Well such is life on a cruise ship where trickery is part of survival.

Crazy Cruise Trivia
Did you know?

During times of war, cruise ships often become war vessels.
In the Falkland Islands conflict between England and Argentina
in the early 1980's England ordered the takeover of
Cunard's QE2, the Canberra
and the Uganda to transport troops.
Unfortunately for the soldiers
the casinos, open bars and
Vegas Extravaganzas
were closed!

Dad visits the ship!

*Backstage for main show
production. I look pretty
professional, but only
pushed a couple of
buttons to open curtain.*

Mail! Mail! Mail!

Stripes Disco — "Man on the Mike".

Gary, the Cruise Director, backstage for bingo game.
Check out the wads of cash.

My co-workers, British Dancers. What a drag!

The "infamous" protein shakes.

Johnny, the disc jockey, poses with me in Stripes Disco.

Denzel, the manic aerobic instructor, clowning around.

Rule #1 – No hanky panky on the ship.

One happy family!
Often crew members would go on outings together.
That's me on the far right. What a hunk! This picture has a combination
of musicians, pursers, child counselors and moi.

Chapter 7
Temptations of the Sea

A couple of hours into a cruise, ladies often notice that something is missing. Their faces all wear a mask of confusion and uncertainty and an edge of nervousness, as they search, feeling a fleeting moment of nakedness like grasping for your wallet in your pocket and finding emptiness. It's not their pocketbook or a piece of clothing missing, rather it's their male partner: a boyfriend or husband led astray. They finally give up the search for their men and just enjoy the company of the other women on the ship who have also become temporary singles. These women often approached me asking the same questions, "Have you seen my husband Harold?" or "Did a man named Bill say he had lost his wife?" In a prophetic tone I would answer, "Follow the sounds of the slot machines and you shall find them."

Casinos are the busiest places on the ship. Open all night long, they buzz with the sounds of hopes and resonate with the whispers of frustration and reality. For crew members the casinos on the ship are off limits, but that's no problem considering many Caribbean ports are famous for their big time casinos, including Puerto Rico and the Bahamas, places we just happened to visit every other week. The casino is the primary destination for many working on the ship, a place they dream about for days after getting their paycheck and their real port-of-call once they step on land. For a couple of months I found myself attracted to this world of gambling, looking to augment my petty salary. It all began after a friend of mine gave me a book on counting cards in black jack, a book I might add was written with scientific confidence and a straightforward plan for immediate wealth. Each day I would read a chapter slowly, concentrating on each word, falling under the spell that this was an actual skill I could learn and eventually perfect winning big bucks in my defeat of the casino lords. Next I would stay up all night with a group of musicians trying to practice counting cards with six decks. As unpolished as I was I still had the courage to try it in the real casinos; but before long realized it was going to take a lot more than reading a couple of pages to make my fortune. Clumsy and unsuccessful, I eventually lost my passion for the casinos, an auspicious event for my bank account.

However, I was an exception on the cruise ship. Often the casinos were full of cruise ship employees all sitting with a thick wad of fresh cash they had just earned on the ship. Each week Carnival employees lined up outside Chris's cubbyhole office and received a small check and a stack of brand new fresh smelling American bills in denominations of twenties, all paper clipped together. It was a bizarre form of payroll and I'm sure some type of corporate legal maneuver that had direct financial benefits for the cruise line. However, for the average ship worker it was the devil's work. A plethora of available cash was a great incentive for gambling and before long those crisp stacks of green were history. It's true that there are great opportunities on a ship to save money; however, temptations like gambling surrounded crew members and often debt was the result.

Another temptation was alcohol. No matter where you turn on a cruise ship you are bound to see a bar or a cocktail waitress. The Ecstasy was a safari of striped fruity concoctions and endless species of beers. Passengers were treated to Rum Swizzle Night their first evening on the ship, champagne bashes with the Captain the following night, and beer drinking competitions the rest of the time. Waiters walked up and down the Promenade deck offering tastes of wine and other free drinks to willing consumers. One might think passengers are doing all the drinking on the ship, but the truth is most of the alcohol on the ship gets consumed on levels below the passenger decks. Walking through the crew living quarters, I couldn't believe the amount of empty beer cans lying around. Much of this drinking is a form of escape for crew members who are homesick or just depressed about their working conditions on the ship.

Alcohol also stands at the center of social life on the ship. My first week on the Ecstasy I had been given a card and a code by Gary which allowed me to get alcohol at any bar for free. This enabled me to get champagne for prizes and beer for the beer-drinking contest. He also mentioned with a wink that I was free to get myself a couple drinks every now and then and not to worry about the tab. And this is exactly what I did.

No matter how hard a person tries on a cruise ship, it's impossible to avoid the sight of food, maybe a temptation more wicked and cunning than alcohol or gambling. Gary performed a song at the beginning of the cruise that detailed how a passenger could start eating in the morning and keep going through the entire day and night. Each night had its own special buffet ranging from pasta nights on Wednesday to desert nights on Thursday to seafood night on Friday. Cruise staff was only allowed to enter the buffets an hour after they were open, but I would often sneak in without anyone knowing who I was and eat with the passengers. Long tables of elaborate ice carvings and food sculptures delighted passengers, each cruise patron passing in front of the creations as one would a Monet or a Renoir in a sacred art museum. My reaction was quite the opposite, these strangely shaped configurations of beef, chicken and pork in the shape of houses, trains and flowers sickened me to the point of nausea.

I couldn't even go close to the buffets after months of eating at each one., Yet, I was a solitaire anomaly in a city of carnivores and scavengers all clawing their way to the food line. There is no doubt that extended time on a ship can do damage to a person's weight. Looking through old pictures of Gary, I almost didn't recognize the thin man in the pictures. He had beefed up considerably in the years he had spent on the ship. A couple of dancers began to battle this problem too; however, for them their job was on the line. All dancers would be weighed once a month to determine whether they were over their required weight, an agreement they had signed in their contract when they joined the ship.

Maybe the most dangerous temptation at sea is wasted time. This is not a problem for most people working 12 to 13 hours a day; however, for cruise staff there is an abundance of free time. Without any hobbies or activities a cruise ship can become a very boring place. How many times can you walk around the ship staring at the same rooms? The dancers also had a lot of time to themselves, but seemed to be pretty adept at finding hedonistic endeavors to partake of, like massages, reading books, sunbathing and watching lots of movies. There was a movie channel on the ship; however, the films were usually bad and remained the same for months at a time. Gary was responsible for ordering new films but was too lazy to get it done, resulting in films like Tom Selleck's *Mr. Baseball* playing for months at a time.

Not a sun worshiper I was obligated to find activities that would keep me busy. One of the first projects I undertook was a weight gain program. The first day I arrived on the ship I weighed only 145 lbs. My thinness reached a state of emergency, many classifying my stomach as concave. Unable to open doors in a single bound I was tired of going through life weak and determined to put on some weight. The cruise ship provided the ideal place to gain weight with a free nautilus and unlimited buffets—it was thin man's utopia. I would lift weights for two hours a day, consume large protein shakes that promised to turn my body into a fighting machine and spend as much time on my bed sleeping or watching movies. The point was to stay motionless and let the pounds build up.

My chocolate shakes put quite a scare into my cabin steward. I had been using my towels to clean the jugs of shakes, leaving my room full of white towels stained with large brown streaks. I could see the disgust on my cabin steward's face as he removed these towels believing me to be a sick animal that was wiping myself with his beautiful white towels, a disgusting but comical thought. Each day after my workout I would go to the crew dining room and eat two of everything, not even pausing to talk to the people sitting next to me. They knew I was on a mission. I wasn't interested in what the food tasted like; rather I wanted large quantities to stuff myself with. Into my mouth I would shove bananas, bread, pasta— anything that would fit. After a month or two my body began to transform from a weakling to this muscular stud. Like the *Incredible Hulk* my skin was stretching, new muscles were blossoming throughout my arms and legs. It was a harvest of tendons. Each day as I walked out of the gym and looked in the mirror I would break into hysterical laughter. I could not believe what I was seeing!!

My next project involved viewing over 400 films during a nine-month period. Certain ports of call have video stores that cater exclusively to crew members renting videos for up to four weeks at a time. Armed with my Roger Ebert review guide I marched directly to the video store once our ship docked in the Bahamas and came back with a stack of ten videos each week. In the jungles of Africa, chimpanzees scream across miles to warn their brethren of a predator. In the wilderness of the M.S. Ecstasy a similar phenomenon occurred with videos. Word spread from cabin to cabin on who had what video and what they were willing to trade for it. It was a bartering system of the highest complexity, video trading that stretched to all levels of the ship. Democracy in its purest form. You might be swapping *Pretty Woman* with Captain Gallo or handing over *Top Gun* to the new child counselor aboard. It was surprising how many crew members had VCRs and how much time was spent holed up in tiny cabins watching Hollywood flicks. I guess it made sense, a true escape from the confined surrounding to the magical places of the movies: deserts, canyons, mountain ranges, and palaces.

Another fascinating phenomenon existed on the ship where crew members' entertainment systems were passed from generation to generation of those who worked on the ship. It was simply too much trouble to haul these items off the ship each time a crew member left or was transferred. Instead a raffle occurred each time a VCR became available. A large sheet was passed around and for ten dollars you could put your name on it. For days the VCR would sit on a table in the crew bar, a statue of glory, provoking sighs and lustful stares from VCR deprived individuals. Finally after about 40 to 50 names were collected they were cut out and thrown in a box. The name chosen won the entertainment system. Everybody won because the departing crew member left with some money in their pocket and didn't have to carry their stuff off, and for ten dollars one lucky shipmate got an entertainment system and a ticket to Hollywood in their cabin.

If I wasn't watching movies or exercising, I could be found reading. The ship library on the Promenade deck had a far better supply of board games than actual books. The novels on the shelves were sparse and placed more for décor than actual use. Along with the comfortable velvet lounging chairs, the library retained a certain shallow dignity and almost always was a quiet sanctuary to gather your thoughts. Passengers brought their novels aboard like their toilet accessories. Packed tight in their suitcases, there was no way they were going to forget them—Steele, Clancy were common names at sea. I always had a curiosity to read the entire Bible cover to cover.

Strange as it may seem I would sit in a chair overlooking the ocean reading verses from Genesis or Leviticus. After reading the Bible for a couple of months, I began to look forward to something different. "How about the complete works of Shakespeare," I thought, and so I began my journey enjoying the poetry of the bard while the beauty of the sea surrounded me. The eloquence of Victorian England experienced among the debauchery of 20th century America was an amusing concept to experience. One thing was for sure, I never saw another traveler pull out William Shakespeare but in a surreal gift from God, the stories and the poetry fit quite nicely into the surroundings.

While the "Tempest" or "A Midsummer Night's Dream," did not draw attention, my Bible was an object of curiosity and a catalyst for conversation. Religion played a curious role aboard the cruise liner. There were no regular religious services on the ship, although for holidays Carnival brought aboard clergy. Within my first couple of months of work, Gary instructed me to hold mass. " I'm not sure that's a possibility," I answered nervously knowing full well that baptism, crucifixions and the Lord's Prayer were not part of my upbringing, rather bar mitzvahs, corned beef and matzo ball soup were more like it. Gary paused, "No worries, just get the suitcase." Shuffling through the supplies closet in the office, I found a black briefcase labeled "church," and quickly opened it to find an instant prayer kit with an assortment of supplies for all your mainstream religions, wooden crosses, wine cups, yarmulkes and a miniature sheet listing the Five Pillars of Islamic Faith. I would give this brief case to the clergy when they came aboard; as well as, a couple of free passes for some tours on the island and in this way was performing the Lord's work cruise ship style. I often was amused watching these clergy run around in their bathing suits drinking beers. They seemed to have more fun than any other passengers, anonymous without their robes, not too different than when we took our uniforms off. The clergy performed marriages on the ship before it left port because marriage at sea was no longer legal. So many couples now tied the knot before the ship ever left port and then conveniently remained aboard for their honeymoon.

Though noble in my sin-free hobbies, the temptations of the cruise world were always present. I witnessed many shipmates fall victim to these temptations. Their time on the cruise ship was often cut short due to the problems and frustrations that arose out of heavy gambling or alcohol use. Relationships turned sour and the pressures of isolation were just too much for many who picked up and left. Still, I persevered, surrounded by companions early in my journey, I held the Devil and his temptations at bay. I didn't need the makeshift cross from the black suitcase or a clove of garlic, just some will power, the Bible, some protein shakes, and a whole lot of Shakespeare.

Crazy Cruise Trivia
Did you know?

Financially strapped steamship companies came up with an idea during Prohibition in the mid 1920's. They began to run their fleets on short trips back and forth to the Bahamas, Havana, and often to nowhere in particular allowing passengers to drink and be merry.

This was the advent of the
Booze Cruise as well as the
"Cruise to Nowhere."

Chapter 8
Moments of Crisis

I had never seen this shade of black before. It stared back at me with a cold and definitive glare and held me prisoner. The darkness enveloped me as I stood alone on the top deck of the cruise ship looking out at a sea of emptiness. This was not the first time I stood here gazing at the waves as they danced a crazy tango with this 70,000 ton hedonistic machine. Often I ended my hectic days of bingo, hairy chest contests, ping-pong, stuffing fiestas, and newlywed games by inhaling the briny air, and for a slice of time savoring the solitude of the ocean and the sheer lack of noise. It was difficult to see where the sky and water met, both overlapping in grays and hiding like a mischievous school kid. Not many passengers walked the decks after 9 p.m., too busy rolling dice in the casino or eating pork chops in the buffets. The competing smells of greasy fries, hot dogs and beer dissipated and was replaced by the cold brisk wind that could only be manufactured by her royal majesty, Mother Nature. I always expected to see a light or something that would signal another life form, but in most cases the only company I had was darkness.

As I walked the Lido deck I was surprised to see more people than usual, as well as the continuous shuffling of crew members as they scurried back and forth. An undercurrent of mumbling caught my attention. There weren't any singles walking around, but rather small groups of people, huddled in circles whispering to themselves, most of them crew. It was like watching that gossip game you play in sixth grade where one person whispers in the next person's ear. Something dramatic had happened on the ship, which the passengers were not privy to. All kinds of thoughts bombarded my head: a storm approaching, a passenger jumped overboard, the ship was sinking, all possibilities except maybe the last one. A couple of co-workers rushed by me up the stairs towards the swimming pool. Their haste was peculiar.

"What's going on?" I asked one of the stewards in the hallway. Breathlessly, he answered, "Micha, you heard, there's going to be an airlift." A rumor had begun to spread around the ship that an emergency medical airlift was to take place. Airlifts did not happen. They were things you heard about. An airlift would mean that a helicopter was coming out to meet the cruise ship in the middle of the ocean to pick up a sick passenger. Most of the passengers would never even know about it, but to the crew it was a momentous occasion that broke up weeks of routine—the circus was coming. I started up the stairs and into the cold air of the night. I climbed up one more level of stairs and stood behind a rope that had been set up to keep a large open area accessible to the medical staff. Passengers walking on the deck had also begun to congregate, sensing that something out of the ordinary was occurring. It was the rubbernecking syndrome you see on highways, explained only by people's morbid curiosity.

Crowds started to form around the ropes, everyone straining on their toes to see what was happening. All eyes were focused at the same dark sky in the distance I had been observing for months, waiting for the spaceship. As I stood among the crew that night, waiting for the helicopter to arrive, I felt like I was part of some Fourth of July celebration waiting for fireworks to appear out of the sky. The only difference was the strange solemnness; each person trying to conceal their deep fear and apprehension of what they were about to witness. The noise level had begun to rise as people became testy, the crowd pushing in on itself and squabbling for a good view.

Without warning, a side door opened and several nurses appeared with a stretcher. Their faces were haggard and crestfallen. Instead of the crisp white uniforms the nurses normally wore, they were dressed in casual sweats and tennis shoes. Whatever had happened, the nurses had been summoned from their sleep. My eyes followed their hands down to a stretcher where a body lay partially covered with a white sheet and several blankets. The only part exposed were two feet sticking out from under the cloth and a small area around the face. This was a crude operation. I hadn't seen many dead things in my life, except for a time I had interned on a farm and saw a big fat cow with its four legs pointing to the sky in rigor mortis, but I couldn't help but compare those two pale feet with the bovines. The sheets draped over the sick passenger had transformed it into a Egyptian mummy. The nurses placed the stretcher on the deck and quickly began tying ropes and knots around its edges. Several other people crowded around the stretcher, making it hard to see. At about the same time, a bright light appeared in the distance and within seconds the familiar sounds of a helicopter could be discerned. The force of the chopper's propellers, along with the ever-present wind, created a loud whirlwind of activity. Each rotation rained a loud piercing boom. A delicate operation took place in front of us as the patient was carefully placed on the deck and positioned for lift off. The helicopter could not land on the ship due to a lack of space, so instead it hovered above the ship and dropped ropes to attach to the patient who would then be lifted and reeled into the helicopter. Every person was glued to the piece of machinery in the sky.

On this particular night the patient was a pregnant passenger who had undergone some complications on the ship and needed to be airlifted to a hospital. The helicopter dropped some cables down to the deck and the nurses worked frantically to attach the patient for the lift. Each second created a more dangerous situation for the helicopter. I grew more tense as time passed and my breathing became labored, as if I were adjusting to a new altitude. As if choreographed, the crowd around the stretcher suddenly took two steps back, and the patient was lifted slowly off the ground, the stretcher remaining horizontal to the deck. The crowd gasped as the little body began to inch away from the deck. Soon the woman was directly above the ocean. I felt nauseous, my stomach in knots; my heart felt as big as a watermelon. For several seconds her lifeless body swayed back and forth in the wind only several feet above the dark unmerciful ocean. Nothing else existed for that brief moment except the little body, the sea and the wind. It reminded me of a David Copperfield magical feat, except this was real and there were no nets beneath this person to catch her. Her body was slowly pulled closer and closer to the gaping doorway in the helicopter, and when it neared the opening, arms grabbed her, pulling her in like a piece of cargo that had finally reached its destination. Before I could blink the helicopter was gone.

For a moment, the crew members and other passengers watching this saga stood quietly, deep in thought. No one stirred. The moment was filled with loneliness as the sky became empty again, with no lights or sound. Where the woman once lay, I saw several people standing with the nurses, most likely family, watching the sky where their loved one had been hovering only moments before. Several of them were embracing while the nurses rubbed their backs to comfort them. What were they thinking? When would they see their loved one again? As I thought about my family, I lost focus on the scene and was reawakened by the crowd beginning to disperse. I returned to my cabin that night not sure if I could sleep after what I had witnessed. I might have drifted off a couple of times, but my brain was in overdrive playing over the momentous scene and flipping death over and over in my mind like an egg, trying to explore all its ramifications, and discover answers to some fear that had welled up within me. I finally negotiated with myself that I would let all my crazy unanswered thoughts stay exactly that—unanswered. As morning arrived, so did the news that the pregnant woman was safe and doing well. For the rest of my time on the Ecstasy I would often return to the spot of the airlift to meditate on what I had seen that night.

Who would take care of me if I had a medical emergency aboard the fun ship? By the time I had earned my stripes as an experienced crew member, which was only a couple of months, I had seen plenty of doctors and nurses come aboard. They were short-term cruisers, similar to rent-a-priest or hired guns, who were offered a free vacation on condition that they be on-call and serve any medical emergencies. You could call them "rent-a-doctor," not all that different from the rent-a-cop stationed outside fraternity house parties. They looked awfully good wearing those little black beepers while they pranced around in their bathing suits, talking on their cell phones, and generally acting obnoxious. The bad news for them was that every 100th cruise, there actually was an emergency where their services were needed and unfortunately some of them did not turn out as well.

Cruise ships are not immune to death, and when death strikes crew members are the first to know about it, that is, after the rent-a-doctor.

There are two rooms on a cruise ship that passengers never see or pray they never see: the brig and the morgue. Cruise ship employees walk by these rooms of doom as a natural part of their daily rounds, although even they can be caught spying into the mysterious windows.

Although some crew end up in the brig if they misbehave, the morgue was for the truly unfortunate. The fact that the morgue was located right down the hall from the cruise staff cabins helped to spark everybody's imagination. Eventually, each cruise staff had to inspect what appeared to be a closet door with the word "morgue" emblazoned on it. Actually, it looked like any other door on the ship, but had a small glass window and a shiny metallic door handle. Close by was a workshop with wood and scrap metal lining the hallway. My imagination ran wild with thoughts of coffins frantically being built late in the night. The room could not have been bigger than six feet by six feet. What if more than one person died on a cruise? What would happen if we hosted an NBA team? Was the room refrigerated? Would we be able to see actual bodies in there?

When word got out that someone had died on the ship, crew members would line the halls to get a peek at the corpse as it was wheeled down the hall to the morgue. This happened rarely but heart attacks and other tragedies did occur and considering each week over 2,000 passengers boarded, it seemed more likely than not. The dancers had a hard time sleeping after watching a body wheeled past their rooms on the way to the morgue. Those nights the regular creeks and groans of the ship often sounded a lot more like the moans and wails of ghosts and goblins. There is even an interesting theory that people board cruise ships with the sole purpose of dying at sea. Cruise ships have always been known as places for the newlywed or the nearly dead. While this may be true on the more luxurious cruise lines that attracted an older crowd, on my cruise ship it was highly unlikely. My ship rarely had senior citizens and when we did it was because they had no idea what Carnival was about and found out too late they booked the wrong cruise. Every once in a while there would be super senior citizen, a Richard Simmons on Viagra who would dance the cruise away, but chances are they were on their 50th cruise and would be back for the 51st pretty soon. Our cruise ship was for living not dying, but if there was any plan to expire on our ship it would have been with style.

Weeks after the airlift the M.S. Ecstasy took its first charter cruise in a long time. A "charter" cruise meant that a private group had rented the entire ship for the week. "Charter" was a favorite word for cruise staff because this basically meant the staff would have that week off. Most of the regular schedule of activities were canceled as the private groups brought on their own entertainment. This week a National Union had chartered the ship and was bringing on delegations from all over the country. The union folks were having a great time. Union members from California were meeting fellow members from Florida and camaraderie flowed like champagne. Passengers were boozing, swimming, sun-tanning; the cruise was off to its usual festive self. Tonight was bingo night. I made my way to the main stage area of the ship where the dancers, looking bored after only ten minutes of work, had already begun selling bingo cards to the passengers.

"All right folks, we are now beginning our final game of the night—a chance to win 500 dollars." My microphone went dead, usually a sign that the ship intercom was about to broadcast some type of news. I waited for the click over the intercom system. It was the Captain's voice that first spoke. He asked for the passengers' attention and introduced the President of the Union who had an announcement. "Jimmy is dead," a scruffy voice mumbled over the intercom. The bluntness of the statement seemed to catch everyone off guard including me. It sounded like Al Capone talking to one of his boys. A rumor had been circulating for the past day that a union member had passed away but it was only hearsay; now it had transformed into truth. Was this some kind of tacky murder mystery cruise where we would have to discover which passenger was the guilty party? Could it be Professor Peacock? I looked out at the crowd of union members with utter disbelief as they began to whisper to one another, much like I had seen that night of the airlift. A visible wave of suspicion washed across the room. People began to hurry out of the hall.

Within minutes the intercom again clicked on. This time it was Gary, who apologized for the last announcement and provided more details on what had transpired and announced a memorial service. A cabin steward had witnessed a passenger sleeping for a long time, but after two days discovered the man was actually dead. I had heard of this happening on a New York City subway car, but not on a cruise out of Miami. The cruise continued as passengers attempted to make the best of a terrible situation.

It was like one long funeral at sea. Some passengers tried to keep partying, but it was obvious that the mood of the trip had taken a dramatic turn. The solemn look in the passengers' eyes told the story. The wild joy of the cruise had been lost and for the last couple of days passengers talked about nothing else but the unfortunate fate of their fellow union member. The cruise lasted forever, but finally we arrived in Miami and not a moment too soon for the crew. I breathed a sigh of relief as I welcomed the new passengers and tried to forget the past week's tragedy at sea.

Passengers on a cruise ship are always looking for fun, trying their hardest to forget the lives they left behind on that thing called land and live a fantasy for seven days on the waters. They are rarely thinking about life threatening illnesses. Most cruisers are focused on one fear, seasickness. It comes down to the eternal question: "Am I going to blow chunks on this ship?" Will my cruise be ruined by an incurable case of nausea and public displays of vomiting? You can't blame them, almost every book on cruising lists all the medicines, patches, and precautions to take. Passengers come armed with the latest technologies to fight this ferocious beast. Pills and patches are the most common means by which passengers attempt to stave off seasickness. I had the same anxiety myself when I first came aboard; however, my worries disappeared quickly after realizing that living on a cruise ship is akin to living in a giant mall. After all, the ship is 13 stories high and the size of several football fields, often taking 15 minutes to walk from one end to the other. You simply don't feel any movement on the Ecstasy. Most passengers don't need all the panaceas, except for maybe the maritime hypochondriacs, which each cruise seemed to have. Now for us working it is hard to escape some rough days at sea. And every once in while there is that rare day that you had feared and on this day even crew go scouring for the patches, Dramamine or anything to fight off the intense nausea.

The Ecstasy had the misfortune to come into Ocho Rios, Jamaica every two weeks, a port that even on the good nights had its share of rocking. Occasionally the rolling was more dramatic, enough to turn my stomach and judging from the amount of passengers walking around the ship, the movement was affecting many more digestive systems than mine. These nights would find me working backstage for the big Las Vegas Style Extravaganza. The ladies running around topless backstage those nights had a little more bounce; in this land of Oz I was the token straight and show nights were very lucky ones for me indeed. While the shaking of the boat added to my enjoyment, I couldn't say the same for them. The dancers threw fits trying to do their routines to the rhythm of the sea. At a certain point, if it got too rough, the dance captain had the right to cancel the show.

One fateful cruise provided the scenario I had feared all along. On that Sunday, several hours before we were to leave port, warnings about a hurricane began to circulate among cruise staff. Everybody in Miami was preparing for the big one, people moving faster than they should, buying groceries for the next millennium. I wasn't too excited about getting on a ship, but the other alternative was to stay ashore and that didn't look too inviting either. The M.S. Ecstasy would be heading right into the eye of the storm so the Captain announced the ship would change its itinerary in order to avoid it. Everything was fine until later that night when the rain began pouring from the dark, angry sky. Soon the wind picked up and the ship began a rhythmic rocking that would go on ceaselessly for the next forty-eight hours. No longer did I feel the security of a 70,000 ton cruise ship. It was feeling more like a fishing trawler. Even topless dancers could not bring a smile to my face.

When I got up in the morning to run an activity, I couldn't even keep my balance on stage. In fact, I was standing at an angle! Lightheaded, I was truly scared for the first time. It didn't help too much that just a week before a sensationalistic television program had featured a story about an ocean liner sinking. I thought planes weren't allowed to show planes crashing on their monitors. I guess the same rule did not apply to ships. There on the TV monitor a huge cruise ship sunk into the ocean about as fast as a piece of cabbage into a trash disposal. It looked like a giant water tornado sucking up the ocean liner into oblivion. "That never happens," a surly passenger commented as I watched the screen in disbelief. "It just did," I answered. Now that we were in rough seas, that scene was on rewind in my mind. Was this going to be our final cruise? No doubt it was a preposterous question to ask, but in the middle of the night as the ship rocked violently back and forth it was more than a passing thought. Passengers were feeling the effects of the storm as most stayed in their cabins or tried to take in the fresh air on the outer decks. Many tried to pretend everything was normal but only a few were able to avoid the sickness spreading like the plague throughout the ship.

Many passengers believed in the magic patch.   Adhered to the person's neck, the patch was supposed to provide enough scopalamine to soothe anxious cruisers. Among the Carnival family, this device was known to be a complete joke and Gary liked to say if you pulled the patch off a passenger they would lose all their air and fly away like a deflated balloon. The patches were definitely not working this particular Monday evening as a showcase of vomiting took place. Everywhere I looked, passengers were hunched over and if they were not actually getting sick their faces signaled the pre-vomiting tension. Usually walking around the ship there would be cordial greetings called out, but on this night each passenger was preoccupied with their own bodily worries. Call in the Red Cross. It was like a city that had been struck by a natural disaster, and if you were roaming the halls there was a good reason you were not lying in your cabin. Either you were going to get supplies or you were on the way to the infirmary.

The cleaners on the ship were busier than ever as they ran from spot to spot performing damage control. This night I dubbed the janitorial crew Noble Nicaraguans. They miraculously didn't jump ship, kept their heads up and worked through most of the night scrubbing the slop of the passengers. Unfortunately for all of us there were just not enough workers to keep up with the rate of seasickness on the ship and this resulted in random vomit landmines spread throughout the passenger areas. It was impossible to take an elevator, for when the doors opened the rancid smell catapulted into the hallway, leaving one no choice but to bolt. The stench made the Smelly Puff Ball seem like a bar of English soap.

Passengers asked anyone they saw in uniform where to go to experience the least amount of movement on the ship. Common knowledge on a ship of the least turbulent place is "middle-middle," meaning the middle cabin on the middle level of the vessel. The following morning as I walked down a crew hallway en route to the dining hall, I noticed a little old man sitting on a beach chair, lost in thought. "Do you need any help," I asked him, knowing he was not crew. "No, I am alright," he mumbled in a sickly voice. "Someone told me this was a good place to sit to avoid the rocking of the ship," he continued. By the time the ship pulled into the port of Puerto Rico, over 20 passengers had decided to pack their bags and disembark. I myself had spent the day before arrival in my room sleeping and praying for this cruise to end. The thought of a new week without nauseous passengers brought a smile to my face.

Luck would have it that the next cruise headed to Jamaica. Though I did not look forward to the waves leaving out of that port, Ocho Rios was beautiful and featured some damn good spicy food and breathtaking scenery. I had planned a casual day of shopping and relaxing and decided to spend the day alone trying to recover from the barf-a-rama theme cruise of the week before. Our stay in Jamaica was considerably less time in port than Puerto Rico or Cozumel, a lesson I learned well that afternoon. The cruise director always announced the time all passengers must return to the ship, but for some reason, with my mind in the clouds, I switched the time of departure with another port. Hours passed and I noticed very few passengers on the streets or lingering in the stores. This was unusual considering the Ecstasy had over 2000 passengers and their presence was strongly felt in a town as small as Ocho Rios. As I strolled along the path that led back to the ship I slowly realized that not only did there seem to be few passengers, there weren't any. The only people I saw were local Jamaicans. Voices of doubt and fear from the roadside warned me, "You're going to miss the boat, man," they said. "Yeah, right," I answered. I didn't take them seriously. As an outsider I was used to teasing by the locals and couldn't actually conceive that I was moments away from missing the boat.

Looking around at the empty walkways I gradually accepted that I might have made a grave mistake. I began to sweat. Suddenly a foghorn blew. The sound sent an electric chill up my body and in that moment reality, fear, and hair-raising pain all came together. I would have to make a mad dash. A few seconds later I heard the roar of the crowd on the top level of the M.S. Ecstasy preparing for departure. In the distance I saw hundreds of small bodies clustered by the railing, looking out at the forests of Jamaica, waving a half-hearted goodbye. My world was about to float away. "Shit!" I yelled in a primal outburst. My heart dropped to my knees and I sprinted towards what seemed to be my home pulling away. The last thing on my mind was staying on this island. Pumping my arms and kicking my legs like a world class sprinter, I prayed I could make it home. "Please God do not leave me!" The crowds' roar got louder. As I got closer I saw that the ropes that held the ship had been removed and it had begun to drift about a foot from land. The crowds' clapping and cheering swelled to a noisy pitch and in my embarrassed state I could only imagine that all 3000 passengers and crew members had recognized me and were laughing hysterically at the idea that the Assistant Cruise Director was going to miss his own boat. I instinctively pulled my baseball cap tighter over my head in a futile attempt to hide my identity.

The gangplanks removed, my only chance was to jump into an open cargo area. I zeroed in on the opening and leaped with all my might, ending up rolling to the ground right next to the Chief of Security, Henry. Big fat Henry, the retired cop from Kentucky recognized me immediately as the smart-aleck food-embezzling Assistant Cruise Director. "Your ID card," he barked at me in his southern drawl. "Here it is," I said solemnly and handed him my future with my head down in humiliation. This was the beginning of a wonderful relationship with Henry. This was normal procedure on the ship, handing over ID cards to security with the understanding that I would have to retrieve it personally from the Captain. Later I would learn, like a diplomat, I had immunity on the ship from many of the rules and regulations. Many crew members would have been fired immediately for barely making the ship's departure. Several dancers had missed the boat during their first week but as "entertainers" they also were privileged to be exempt from certain rules and were flown aboard at the next port. I was in no real danger, though I was scared shitless and later that night Gary giggled and playfully threw my ID back at me. "Try not to do that again." Before long the incident was forgotten.

Just as important as getting on the boat, was getting off. Some crew called it "going stir crazy," others simply said the only way to keep your sanity was to get back on land and sample normal life. Each Sunday in Miami provided this sliver of normalcy and more importantly, an escape from ship life. I was like a Pavlovian dog, for as the port of Miami neared, my whole body shivered with childish excitement. A giant present awaited me in Miami. It was simply an American city full of all the pleasures I had grown accustomed to, ranging from movies, to shopping malls and the Golden Arches. It was capitalism with all its faults, faults I had grown to love and after some time away from my homeland, I now coveted. Of course, there was no guarantee that crew members would actually be allowed off the ship. Normal protocol called for crew members to be cleared off the ship at noon and have most of the day off in Miami. The quicker the passengers got off, the quicker the crew could follow. Sometimes due to passport problems or slow disembarkation for passengers, the crew was held up, but it was never for too long.

One of those typical Sundays turned out to be not so ordinary. For some strange unexplained reason ship staff were told they might not be able to get off the ship 'til 2 p.m. Furious with the bureaucracy of the port, this was the last news I needed to hear. I had been spending time with my high school friend Sandy for months now. Our routine was blissful: Sandy, completing a clerkship for a Judge in Miami, would pick me up at the port, and we would whiz off for day excursions as he would catch me up on all the gossip of our friends. Since I already had plans to meet Sandy at 12:30 p.m., I did not plan to stay aboard the ship. By noon, several hundred crew members crowded the lower level deck near the exit of the ship, anxiously awaiting permission to get off. I had been working in the office in the morning and still had my uniform on. As my desperation increased, I began to think of schemes that would get me off the ship. I was aware that the fine for having Carnival staff leave the ship before clearance was in the thousands of dollars, but at the moment I was so enraged, all I wanted to do was beat the system. Each new delay set off a chorus of angry sighs from crew members. It was starting to look like an angry lynch mob.

During Sunday mornings it was routine for me to pass into the terminal from the ship in order to check on passengers or run official papers to the office. Once in the terminal it was only one simple turn and I could be on an escalator heading to the street. Hustling back to my cabin, I undressed and put on some shorts and a T-shirt underneath my uniform. This was the closest I had come to Clint Eastwood in *Escape From Alcatraz*, but I was going to bust out. Grabbing some papers from my desk, I rushed by some security guards and entered the terminal area. I pretended to be in a hurry and looked very businesslike, and when I stepped on the escalator I quickly removed my starched work shirt and slipped on a T-shirt. I would have set off any lie detector close by with my body in overdrive, sweat and fear coating my skin. A couple more steps and I would be free. By the time I arrived at street level I looked like any other passenger. Sandy was waiting in the parking lot looking confused. I quickened my steps. As I walked briskly towards my get-away car, I glanced back at the cruise ship and had a hard time believing what I had just done. No one would ever know I was gone. All I could think about was the hundreds of frustrated crew members standing on the deck waiting for permission to get off. Basking in the exhilaration of the moment, I raised my arms to the sky and gently whispered the sweet word "Victory." I had overcome my latest crisis, and for a few hours now I could enjoy the sun and sounds of South Beach. Soon I would face my largest crisis of all—one that would develop within me and sneak up closer each day until it had to be faced.

Crazy Cruise Trivia
Did you know?

Those strange initials before cruise ship titles
actually stand for something.
M.S. – Motor Ship
T.T.S. – Twin Turbine Screw
T.S. – Turbo Ship
M.V. – Motor Vessel
S.S. – Steamship

Chapter 9
Honeymoon Blues

I was doing the cha-cha with the big white whale I had first met so long ago that fateful first day at the Port of Miami. Life on the ship was a honeymoon; after all, I spent most of my time playing while devoting very few hours to work. Yet all honeymoons must come to an end, and by the seventh month of my journey I was beginning to experience the blues. Emotionally I was beginning to suffer as each day began to drag. One night I found myself gasping for air. I quickly felt my collar to see if it needed loosening, but that did not seem to be the problem. I quickly ran up the stairs until I was outside near the pool staring at the sky and taking long deep breaths. "What was happening to me?" It felt like a mixture between claustrophobia and choking on a chicken bone. Spending so much time below the deck I began to crave fresh air. For a couple of weeks I sat on the deck each night reading books to avoid this feeling of claustrophobia. My patience was at an all-time low as I began to take some of my frustrations out on passengers. I was rushing through my activities. One afternoon during the Beer Drinking Competition, I found myself screaming at a pack of wild college kids. For months I had entertained passengers with jokes, but now I felt like I was dealing with school children. As my fuse got shorter I realized my time for departure was approaching.

The dining room was also beginning to become a very serious concern for me as I began skipping meals. I just could not stand to look at

111

the food anymore. My appetite was non-existent. Many passengers have the mistaken impression that crew members eat the same food they do, yet the only time I ate in the passenger dining room was when I had a guest aboard for the week. Week after week I ate in the cruise staff dining room, one of several dining rooms serving meals for crew members. The most elaborate crew dining room, with waiter service and food similar to what the passengers ate, was the officer dining room. The Captain could be found here eating in the plush dining room except on nights when he was required to make appearances for the passengers. All of the captains I knew were on the shy side, and unlike on television dreaded going up to make public appearances. So much for Captain Stubing! The largest dining room was for most of the crew and was buffet style. The food resembled slop. This dining room was always alive with televisions blaring the soccer games from around the world.

The dining room I ate in was for cruise staff and had waiter service. These were the waiters in training and for now we were the guinea pigs. More to the point, I felt as if I was eating guinea pigs. For a short time the food was bearable and, through bribes, I was able to get adequate service. I would give my waiter a dollar or two before the meal and would receive good service. One of the great treats on the cruise ship is room service which is available to passengers at all times and coveted by crew. Crew members are strictly forbidden to order room service; however, when I was working in the office an archaic loophole penned into the ship constitution by the Cruise Director allowed me to dial the forbidden number. Grilled cheese sandwiches became my devilish secret. When I stopped going to meals I realized I would have to consider getting off the ship solely for the purpose of eating again.

In addition to suffering from the food dilemma, I soon found myself becoming a prisoner of time. As a crew member your life is always restricted by the hours the ship is in port. Checking your watch becomes a part of your life. Sometimes in port you lose yourself in whatever you are doing, but sooner or later the fun must come to an end so you can rejoin the ship. Gary had given me permission to stay in certain ports overnight and rejoin the ship the next day. This could be done with ports like Puerto Rico and the Virgin Islands because they were geographically so close that a plane could get me there in less than an hour. I never took him up on the offer but was close to doing it by the time I got off the ship.

I reached a turning point in my frustration when the ship began to feel like prison. When I actually stopped to think about the similarities, I was astonished. Distrust was at a very high level. I began to notice items missing from my room and stood guard over my laundry. Over 800 crew members create an environment where it is impossible to know everyone, and a great deal of stealing goes on. Like a prison, a black market existed on the ship where items such as magazines and cigarettes could be bought from certain crew members. Of course, these items were legal, but many crew members rarely got off the ship and to them these items were worth paying a little extra for.

Almost all of the crew were men and the few women that existed experienced a lot of hassle due to this fact. The sexual frustration among crew members was evident in the way the men looked at the few women crew members as they walked down the hallways. Their stare was primitive and filled with ravenous hunger. Imagine a prison movie as a sexy lady dressed in tight shorts walks down the corridor. Now imagine the same prison movie but the sexy lady is a man with a beard, a wart and a long nose. On the cruise ship both would get stares; that's how bad it was. These few women were stared at as if they were some foreign creature on the ship. Every once in a while a special performance, put on by the cruise staff, would entertain the crew members. Charla would put on her sexy costumes and sing a couple of songs causing the hundreds of crew members to explode in shouts and screams. The scene could have easily been a group of soldiers during a war who hadn't seen women for months. Topping all this was dining slop-style which couldn't have been too different from prison. Security guards were always watching the crew waiting for them to break some rule. For brief moments all of these elements came together and voila, the cruise ship had become a prison at sea.

My longing for home became a daily thought. As each day dragged on I fantasized about living in a city and doing all the things that used to be so normal in my life. I wanted to sit at a cafe late at night, watch a baseball game, go to a concert, cook my own meals. I wanted a normal life again. Like all honeymooners I was beginning to notice the warts of this beautiful cruise line experience. I started off as Assistant Cruise Director and had been turned into a caged animal. It was only a matter of time before I would set myself free.

Crazy Cruise Trivia
Did you know?

Retired cruise ships never die they just become
… floating hotels.
The Queen Mary,
one the most luxurious cruise liners of its time
is a sightseeing attraction and hotel in Long Beach, California.

Chapter 10
Is There Life After Cruising?

I couldn't believe the news. Gary was leaving. He was being transferred to another ship and in a matter of days I would meet his replacement, Bobby. As I said good-bye to Gary that Sunday I realized my whole routine on the cruise ship would change; the good times were over. Bobby arrived on the scene with a reputation that already stunk. After his first meeting with the cruise staff I was not looking forward to my future on the ship. A large man with very little hair, Bobby was a combination of arrogance and bad taste. No matter how much he tried, Bobby was just not a likable man. This was a man who really believed himself to be funny. Listening to Bobby, I couldn't help but think he had an inferiority complex the size of Texas. The cruise staff had no choice but to accept him, although for the rest of his time on the ship very few dancers took the time to speak to him. The unspoken policy was to just leave him alone and engage in conversation only when absolutely necessary. This was the course of action I took, often leaving notes for him under his door and avoiding contact whenever possible.

My resentment for him increased as my responsibilities changed. Whereas, Gary ran most of the big events on the ship, Bobby liked to delegate as much responsibility into the hands of the cruise staff. I was now required to attend events that had no need for me, such as the Captain's cocktail party where I would stand in the corner for two hours with no real

115

purpose. Bobby was terribly paranoid and always hiding somewhere close to my activity to see if I got there on time. He would often call me into his office to chastise me for things I had said during my activities. When I watched Bobby in front of the passengers I wondered how a man of his demeanor could become a cruise director for a ship of 3000 passengers. I figured if I stuck my time out on the ship I would easily become a cruise director. However, that was a thought as far away as the moon as I struggled to deal with my great frustration on the ship. Soon Bobby became just another aggravation that pushed me to the point of resignation.

By now I was the grandfather on the ship having outlived generations of crew members. I could walk the ship blindfolded. Grumbling like an old man, and burnt out beyond repair, I collapsed at my desk one late night to write my letter of resignation. In the morning I dropped it in the mail and began packing my bags. The following Sunday as we arrived in Miami I was greeted by the Entertainment Director of Carnival. "Micha, I want to urge you to stay a little longer," he said. "No, I'm sorry but I am going to be leaving in two weeks," I assured him. Sensing that I was not going to be very cooperative, Charles, the man who I had once sat down with for hours talking about golf, took the offensive. He caught me off guard by questioning my commitment to the cruise line. "You really don't give a fuck?" he said. "No, I guess I don't." I answered with little hesitation. I didn't mean to be belligerent or frivolous. I just could not see myself staying one day longer than the two weeks I had already promised. I was a sick man. I was leaving and I was not coming back. In order to avoid a nervous breakdown I had to leave, and there was no haggling to be done.

By this time cruises had become routine. I could still remember my first when I stood on the deck and watched Miami disappear into the sunset. In many ways I viewed all of my cruises as one big cruise. I had often envisioned my year on the ship as a trip out to sea, and when I returned I would have a new perspective on who I was and what I wanted out of life. This was a lot to ask but as my last cruise came to an end I was certain I had learned many valuable lessons. Most of all, I walked away with a much greater appreciation of the day-to-day tasks that people take for granted. I looked with enthusiasm to living in a city and appreciating simple life. I was awakened to the great privileges I was entitled to purely because I was an American and was thankful for the great freedom I would have once I left the ship. I was a richer person in my knowledge of literature and film, and had gained about twenty pounds. Fearless of heavy winds or heavy doors, I was a much more confident person stepping off the ship my final time and deeply grateful for the opportunity to be part of this unique cruise world.

Now I was on my final cruise and once again I enjoyed the delightful view of Miami as the cruise ship sailed away. Each day I felt a unique combination of nostalgia and novelty. Every step I took reminded me of a different experience and yet much of my time on this cruise seemed new and fresh. I had turned the ship into my home and would soon leave this family. As I looked out toward the ocean, I was able to put aside my overwhelming desire to get off and savor the sensational opportunity. I had lived a dream. Each night I would pack away a couple items in my room. The rest of my free time was embracing my crew mates with big hugs and saying good-byes to all of my friends on the ship. I took the opportunity at the ports to take certain dancers out to dinner and collect phone numbers and addresses. The reality was I would not see many of these people again. For months I had been preparing other crew members to get off the ship. It was hard to believe my time had arrived.

Sunday morning arrived. I dressed myself with frenzied excitement and energy. All crew members waiting to leave had to gather at a certain time to fill out the required paper work. I watched the passengers leaving knowing that in less than an hour I would be driving around Miami and my cruise experience would be a memory. The crew purser asked for our attention. We would need to follow him down the hallway and into the cargo area where he would escort us to the immigration officials and then off the ship. As I walked off the ship that day I truly felt like a man who had been freed of a tremendous burden. I couldn't walk fast enough. Looking back, I realize my emotions were more a result of the moment and not of the total experience. Picking up the boxes I had packed most of my belongings in, I stepped into a terminal area where an official checked our baggage, possibly for stolen plastic cruise trophies or other contraband. I had heard horror stories about crew members having to pay large sums of money for electrical equipment they were taking off the ship. The officials waved me through. I took a couple of short steps into the sun of Miami. As I stood on the dock looking back at the beast in the sea, I whispered "Adios Amigo." I turned and caught a taxi. After 11 months at sea I was heading home.

My adjustment to land life began on a sour note. I had agreed to accompany Johnny who was driving up the coast to Boston. As we neared the town of Savannah, Georgia, Johnny suggested we get a hotel in town for the night. This was a bit off our path but I agreed. Exhausted, we picked the first hotel we found, left most of our stuff in the car and sank into our beds. In the morning, as Johnny showered, I went out to the car to get my electric shaver. As I approached the car, the back window appeared to look like tin foil. As I got closer my eyes met the image of shattered glass. The car had been robbed. Suddenly I had a horrible feeling deep in my gut. I had left my briefcase full of bank checks and official papers in the car. All of my savings were in that briefcase. "I'm screwed," I kept saying to myself as I searched for the briefcase. It was gone. I panicked for an hour or so before I realized I had taken several of the most important checks out before leaving Miami, and I had not lost anything of value except for some letters. These letters were mostly from Project Random. I searched the grounds of the hotel hoping the thieves had tossed these letters but finally had to give up. After waiting a couple of hours for the window to be fixed we waved a resentful good-bye to Savannah.

Soon I was home. Always wondering where the ship was at every particular moment, I was no better than a broken-hearted lover. Sundays at 4 p.m. always caused an instinctual pull within my mind to report to the ship or I would be left on land. It felt weird to be standing on land after 4 p.m. on Sundays. I had planned to return to Washington D.C. and then move to New York City. For the first couple of weeks I caught up with old friends, sharing the stories of my journey. I was surprised at the great excitement and curiosity about my time on the ship. After a couple of weeks of sharing my stories I began to settle into my new life. The experiences of the ship seemed further and further away. The struggles of starting over were overwhelming at first. Apartments, car payments, grocery shopping, it all felt burdensome. After all, I never had to worry about this stuff on the ship. During the rough times I often thought of returning to the cruise ship. The temptation was so sweet but I knew I would only be running away. I would be putting my life on hold. The cruise ship provided a wonderful chapter in my life but the rest of the book remains to be written. Every now and then while walking down the streets of New York I will stroll by a travel agency window with a miniature model of cruise ship on display, sometimes even the M.S. Ecstasy. Slowly I creep up to the glass, stop and stare and whisper to myself in a voice barely audible to the hustling New Yorkers brushing by me, "That was me, that was me."

Crazy Cruise Trivia
Did you know?

Need a cruise ship? Here are some price tags.

Carnival Spirit – Carnival Cruise Lines – 375 Million

Golden Princess – Princess Cruise Lines – 450 Million

Adventure of the Seas – Royal Caribbean
Cruise Lines – 550 Million

Norwegian Sun – Norwegian Cruise Lines – 332 Million

Sandpiper Kayak – $299

Discovery Scout Wooden Canoe – $779

J.C. Hawaii Surfboard – $425

Ten Commandments of Cruising

1 GET ON, LIVE IT UP, GET OFF
The best way to enjoy life on a cruise ship is not to stay on too long. Six months to a year is plenty of time to appreciate the experience, any longer and you may become "stir crazy."

2 GET OFF THE SHIP WHENEVER YOU CAN
In order to balance a healthy lifestyle, it is wise to spend as much time away from the ship as possible. If there is land run to it!

3 HAVE GOALS
Depending on your position you may have a lot of time to yourself. In order to avoid boredom make sure you have projects and hobbies to fill your time.

4 EAT OUT AT EVERY PORT
The food will get sick pretty quickly and the only way to deal with it is to have your own supply or eat out often.

5 ALWAYS BE FRIENDLY TO CREW
Cruise ships are not good places to build up enemies. You never know when you will need a favor.

6 AVOID ALCOHOL AND GAMBLING

These are the quickest ways to blow your savings on the ship. The temptations are great and the results disastrous.

7 DON'T FORGET THE PASSENGERS

Crew members tend to ignore the passengers; however, the interesting people you can meet may surprise you. Also it provides you a way to stay in touch with the world outside the cruise ship.

8 ENJOY THE SEA, MOON, AND STARS

Life on a cruise ship surrounds you with beautiful nature. Make sure to look for the dolphins and spend some nights on deck looking at the stars. It's well worth it.

9 STAY SUSPICIOUS

The cruise ship is not a trusting environment. Always stay on guard.

10 DEVELOP A FEW CLOSE FRIENDS

A support system can make or break you on a ship. Look for a few trusted friends and keep them close.

Addendum

The resumé I used to get my job with Carnival Cruise Lines.

Micha Berman
736 22nd St. #405
Washington D.C 20037
(202) 676-2534

Dear Mr. Zwick:

In a few months I will graduate from George Washington University where I am doing my graduate work after receiving my B.A. from the University of Virginia. While at the University of Virginia I was an active member of Alpha Epsilon Pi and am still a strong supporter of the fraternity today. After some hard thinking I have decided that my skills of oral communication and creative programming would best be put to use as a cruise staff member on a cruise ship.

I located your name in the Alpha Epsilon Pi Fraternity Alumni Directory and because of my interest in the New York area thought you would be a good person to ask for advice.

The position of a cruise staff member fits my personality and interests very well and most important I am excited about the prospect of working on a ship and traveling to new places. After spending hours looking through this Alumni book it is clear to me that not many AEPI alumni have entered into the field I am interested in, yet I am still hopeful that due to the time you have spent in New York you might know people who are currently employed in this area and would be helpful to talk to.

I have included my resume so that you can see some of my past accomplishments and learn a little about who I am. I want to thank you for taking the time to read my letter and let you know that I greatly appreciate any information you could provide.

From the time I have spent in Manhattan (I have visited Manhattan quite a few times in the last year to see a good friend of mine who lives in the Upper West Side near Columbia University) I can truly say that I would be thrilled to find an opportunity in such an exciting part of the country. Thank you very much and I look forward to hearing from you soon.

Sincerely,

Micha Berman

One of the letters I sent out in Project Random connecting with college fraternity brothers across the country.

From the desk of

OCTOBER 14, 1999

TOMMY DIGEROLAMO

DEAR MICHA,

GUESS WHO? I TOOK THE COURSE YOU TAUGHT @ NYU ENTITLED "HOW TO GET A JOB ON A CRUISE SHIP" BACK IN SPRING I GUESS. GUESS WHAT? YOU ARE NOW HEARING FROM THE NEWEST "ENTERTAINMENT HOST" ON-BOARD "CELEBRITY CRUISES" MV ZENITH! EFFECTIVE 11/21/99 MY ROUTE WILL INCLUDE 2 WEEK SAILINGS OUT OF SAN JUAN TO CARIBBEAN TO SOUTH AMERICA TO MEXICO & FINISHING IN SAN DIEGO. THE SPRING WILL TAKE ME NEW YORK TO BERMUDA BARRING ANY CHANGES. I HAVE A 6 MONTH CONTRACT THEN 6 WEEKS OFF ETC. YOU PROBABLY REMEMBER HOW IT WORKS. I CONTACTED ADELE & TOLD HER AS WELL (FELLOW CLASS ATTENDEE). I JUST WANTED TO SAY THANKS AGAIN FOR ALL YOUR INPUT IN MAKING MY DREAM JOB COME TRUE. ALSO FOR YOUR RECOMMENDATION LETTER & YOUR MANUSCRIPT. I TOLD YOU THAT I READ IT & REALLY ENJOYED THE VOYAGE IT BROUGHT ME THROUGH. HOW ARE THINGS GOING WITH THE MANUSCRIPT? ANY PUBLISHING LEADS YET? I'LL SEND YOU MY ADDRESS ON THE HIGH SEAS IF YOU WANT TO STAY IN TOUCH. UNTIL THEN HERE'S TO SMOOTH SAILING, FOLLOWING WINDS, & SAFE RETURNS - BON VOYAGE -

CHAMPAGNE WISHES & CAVIAR DREAMS AWAIT!

BEST REGARDS -

Tommy DiGerolamo

A letter from a student who took my cruise class at NYU.

MICHA BERMAN currently resides in Marin County, north of San Francisco, with his wife and two sons and continues to use his microphone skills honed on the cruise ship as a professional voice-over artist. He is a graduate of the University of Virginia and holds a Masters of Social Work from New York University and a Masters of Political Science from George Washington University. For several years he taught a class on "How to Get a Job on a Cruise Ship," as an Adjunct Professor at New York University and has published magazine articles on how to break into the cruise industry. His resumé includes short stints in strange, smelly places including a dairy farm, law school, the United States Congress, and the Tony Awards. He spends most of his time changing poopy diapers, and buying lottery tickets. He has no immediate plans for any cruises.

Printed in the United States
124878LV00006B/253-261/P